MATHEMATICAL PROBLEM-SOLVING WITH THE MICROCOMPUTER

Dr. Stephen L. Snover, an assistant professor of mathematics and computer science at the University of Hartford in West Hartford, Connecticut, was an author for the Boston University Mathematics Project and has written articles on topics in both mathematics and computer science.

Dr. Mark A. Spikell, a mathematics educator and chairman of the Department of Education at George Mason University in Fairfax, Virginia, has co-written the books *Problem Solving in the Mathematics Laboratory* and *Multibase Activities.*

Jointly they have written three other books published by Prentice-Hall, *How to Program Your Programmable Calculator, Brain Ticklers,* and *Programming the TI–55 Slide Rule Calculator.*

MATHEMATICAL PROBLEM-SOLVING

WITH THE

MICROCOMPUTER

Projects to Increase Your
BASIC
Programming Skill

Stephen L. Snover

Mark A. Spikell

A SPECTRUM BOOK

Prentice-Hall, Inc., Englewood Cliffs, New Jersey 07632

Library of Congress Cataloging in Publication Data

Snover, Stephen L.
  Mathematical problem-solving with the microcomputer.

  (A Spectrum Book)
  Includes index.
    1. Microcomputers — Programming.   2. Basic (Computer
program language).   3. Problem solving — Data processing.
I. Spikell, Mark A.   II. Title.
QA76.6.S6167   001.64   82-360
ISBN 0-13-561829-0   AACR2
ISBN 0-13-561811-8 (pbk.)

This Spectrum Book can be made available to businesses and
organizations at a special discount when ordered in large
quantities. For more information, contact: Prentice-Hall,
Inc.; General Publishing Division, Special Sales;
Englewood Cliffs, New Jersey 07632.

10   9   8   7   6   5   4   3   2   1

Editorial/production supervision by Eric Newman
Cover design by Jeannette Jacobs
Manufacturing buyer: Barbara A. Frick

0-13-561829-0

0-13-561811-8 {PBK.}

Prentice-Hall International, Inc., *London*
Prentice-Hall of Australia Pty. Limited, *Sydney*
Prentice-Hall Canada, Inc., *Toronto*
Prentice-Hall of India Private Limited, *New Delhi*
Prentice-Hall of Japan, Inc., *Tokyo*
Prentice-Hall of Southeast Asia Pte. Ltd., *Singapore*
Whitehall Books Limited, *Wellington, New Zealand*

CONTENTS

III

BASIC PROGRAM SOLUTIONS
TO THE PROBLEMS, 135

IV

NUMERICAL ANSWERS TO THE PROBLEMS, 147

V

BASIC PROGRAM SOLUTIONS
TO THE EXTENSIONS, 153

VI
NUMERICAL ANSWERS
TO THE EXTENSIONS, 181

PREFACE

For all practical purposes, microcomputers were first available commercially in 1977. By the early 1980s there were more than 500,000 of these computing machines in homes, schools, and offices. Some experts predict that by the year 2000 virtually every person will have his or her own personal computer (or *microcomputer*, as they are often called).

Whether the experts' predictions come true or not, there is little doubt that the microcomputer has already had a significant impact on our lives. These machines make it possible for virtually anyone to have, at an ever-decreasing cost, the powerful computing and problem-solving capacity usually thought to be available only to the scientific or business communities.

One can only imagine the possible implications of having computer technology available to millions of people rather than thousands. Come what may, it seems reasonable to infer that increasing numbers of people need and will want to know more about computers in general and what they can and cannot do.

This book gives readers an idea or feeling for some of the kinds of numerical problems that can be solved with a microcomputer. It also provides ample opportunity for individuals to develop or enhance programming and problem-solving skills. Finally, it permits the reader to gain some insight into both the power and the limitations of computer technology.

WHO IS THIS BOOK FOR?

This book is written for anyone who has access to or who owns a microcomputer or computer, including the following:

- beginning computer programmers
- computer hobbyists
- microcomputer owners
- teachers of computer programming
- puzzle enthusiasts
- computer science teachers
- mathematics and science students
- gift-giving friends and relatives

WHAT IS THE PURPOSE OF THE BOOK?

The purpose of this book is to enable readers to:

- experience mathematical problem-solving using a computer
- learn how to adapt a working program to solve a related problem
- get a feeling for the range of numerical problems that can be solved by the computer
- gain insight into the power and limitations of the computer in computational problems
- have a resource collection of interesting numerical problems for computer solution

WHICH COMPUTER
SHOULD I USE WITH THIS BOOK?

This book has been written for use with any computer with BASIC and at least 1K of memory. For example, you can use any of these microcomputers:

- Apple II or Apple III
- TRS-80 Model I, II, or III
- ATARI 400 or ATARI 800
- Commodore PET
- Ohio Scientific Challenger
- Radio Shack hand-held computer
- TI 99/4
- Sinclair ZX80

- Compucolor II
- Exidy Sorcerer

and essentially all other small and large machines.

HOW MUCH MATHEMATICS
OR COMPUTER PROGRAMMING
DO I NEED TO KNOW?

Most of the problems in this book require no more mathematics than is customarily taught in first-year algebra and no more computer programming than a simple working knowledge of beginning BASIC. However,

- If any more advanced mathematics is needed, it is explained in the text and presented in the accompanying program.
- If more advanced BASIC programming techniques are used, they are carefully explained in the text.

ACKNOWLEDGMENTS

We wish to thank several people for their help in preparing this book. First, thanks to Judith Campbell-Reed for her patience and creative artwork. Her artistic flair does much to make this a visually appealing book. Second, thanks to John E. Hunger and his colleagues for useful brainstorming on the packaging and titling of this book. John's editorial support for this and other joint projects has always been appreciated, as has the able assistance of his assistant, Lou-Ann E. Leahy-O'Rourke. Third, thanks to Mark Schmidt for his help in preparing the program listings that appear in this book. We also extend special thanks to Laurie and J.B. for their continued support.

MATHEMATICAL PROBLEM-SOLVING WITH THE MICROCOMPUTER

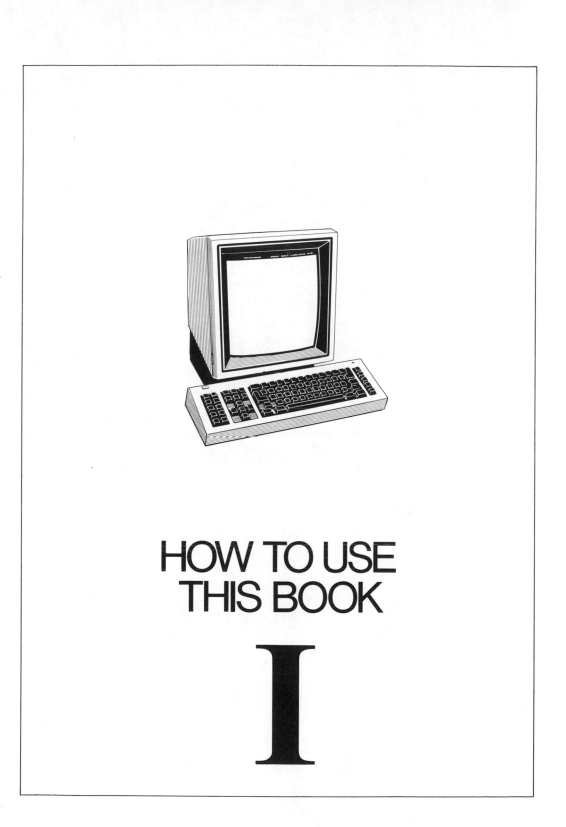

HOW TO USE
THIS BOOK

I

INTRODUCTION

Computers! Everywhere you turn, your life is increasingly affected by these electronic marvels. Airlines rely on computers to handle reservations; banks rely on computers to keep track of deposits and withdrawals; hospitals rely on computers to store medical records; large corporations rely on computers to issue employee paychecks; the list is endless.

Because computers are so pervasive in society, knowing something about how they work and how they can be used to solve problems is important information for the educated citizen. But how best does one learn about computers—by reading about them? Not likely, in our opinion. We believe that one learns the potential and power of computers by using them. And we are convinced that one learns best by actively participating in the learning process (doing) rather than passively participating (reading or listening).

To help you obtain a feeling for how computers solve various problems, we want you to actually write computer programs. That is why we designed this book around a collection of interesting mathematical (numerical) problems that you can solve with a computer. By using this book and exploring the problems, you will learn, we are confident, a great deal about computers, programming, and problem solving. Furthermore, you will experience our philosophy that people learn by doing and learn even more by doing and having fun at the same time.

PURPOSE OF THE BOOK

We have written this book so that you can use it for a number of different purposes. On the one hand, we want you to gain pleasure out of solving these problems with your computer. Each of the problems is designed to be solved in twenty to thirty minutes. And for each problem, there are several suggested extensions that you might explore. In the process, we hope you will gain insight into how to utilize your computer to help you solve problems. On the other hand, we hope you will be able to review and practice your BASIC computer programming skills by writing programs of your own and by seeing and running programs we present. Moreover, we think you will pick up new BASIC skills, such as ones related to updating or adapting BASIC programs to get them to perform related tasks. In particular, we hope you will gain a better feeling for the power and limitations of your computer as a mathematical problem-solving tool while having fun, too.

USING THE BOOK
WITH A VARIETY OF MACHINES

We selected and designed problems for this book so that any computer having the BASIC computer language could be used. If you have access to or own a microcomputer (e.g., the Apple, ATARI, PET, TRS-80, etc.), you will find that these problems can be readily solved on these machines. Even small hand-held computers with only 1K of memory can be used.

The program listings presented either as core programs or problem solutions are written with BASIC instructions that are general enough to work on virtually every computer that uses a form of the BASIC language. We avoided instructions that work on only one or some computers so that you could use this book with any machine. Although many other books claim that you can *easily* modify any of these programs to run on your machine, we have discovered that it is usually far from easy. Thus, we really designed our book so that you do not need to make any modifications at all to get these programs to work on your machine. We trust that the extra effort on our part will mean less frustration and more benefit for you.

FORMAT OF THE BOOK

This book is designed in a six-part format so that you will have maximum flexibility to use it for educational or recreational purposes. The six parts are:

Part I: How to Use This Book
Part II: Problems, Core Programs, Modification Suggestions, and Extensions
Part III: BASIC Program Solutions to the Problems
Part IV: Numerical Answers to the Problems
Part V: BASIC Program Solutions to the Extensions
Part VI: Numerical Answers to the Extensions

Although many books are available that give problems to solve or computer programs to run, we know of no other book quite like this one. The collection of problems for computer solution in Part II is presented in a unique way. We give each problem, with a cartoon for aesthetic appeal. Then we present a short BASIC program that focuses on a specific idea fundamental to the solution of that problem. Next, we present suggestions on how you can use the short program as the core of a larger program in BASIC that will actually give the solution. Also, we provide several extensions to each problem so that you can have more practice at modifying programs to solve related tasks and to provide more experience with the use of the computer as a problem-solving tool. Finally, we include a blank page so that you can have a space to write your program, record extensions of your own, or make other notes. This unusual presentation should be flexible enough to enable you to use this book in a variety of ways.

In Parts III through VI, we present BASIC programs and numerical solutions to all the problems and extensions from Part II. We have separated the programs from the corresponding numerical solutions for an important reason—to provide even more flexibility of use. If you enjoy the challenge of writing your own programs, you can consult just the numerical answers in Parts IV or VI to verify the accuracy of your work. Or, if you wish to consult or copy the programs in Parts III and V, the numerical solutions will not be given away before you have a chance to enter and run these programs.

If you plan to use any of our core programs or modification suggestions, we encourage you to read the rest of this introductory chapter. In the next section, we proceed step by step through the solution of a sample problem. This will help you discover by "doing" how you can use our core programs and suggestions in designing a BASIC program to solve any of the problems in this book.

A SAMPLE PROBLEM

On the next page is a statement of Mad Mary's Problem, with a cartoon. We hope you will find the cartoon accompanying each problem an attractive feature to stimulate your interest in solving the problem.

Mad Mary's Problem

Mad Mary is an amateur mathematician and a manufacturer of children's toys. She needed to give product codes to a set of six plastic squares, parts for one of these toys, and decided to choose the product codes according to a mathematical rule so that she could easily remember the codes. She noted that the square of the number 25 is 625 and 625 ends in the number 25 itself. So she decided to number one of the plastic squares with the product code 25. In fact, she discovered that there are exactly six numbers of less than 400 that have the same property—the number itself is the rightmost part of its square. So she numbered each of the six plastic squares with those six numbers. What were her choices?

Next, we present a short BASIC program that you can use as the core of a larger program to solve Mad Mary's Problem. Together with the BASIC core program, there is an explanation of what it does and how it is fundamental to the solution of the problem. (Within the problems themselves in Part II, this "Core Program" is referred to as "part A" for the sake of brevity.)

Core Program

☐ To help you find the six numbers, following is a program to test whether any given number appears as the rightmost part of its square.

```
 10 INPUT N
 20 FOR I=1 TO 9
 30    D=I
 40    IF N<10^I THEN 60
 50 NEXT I
 60 S=N*N
 70 P=INT(10^D+.5)
 80 T=S-P*INT(S/P)
 90 IF T=N THEN 120
100 PRINT N;" IS NOT ";
110 GOTO 130
120 PRINT N;" IS ";
130 PRINT "THE RIGHT-MOST PART OF ";S
140 END
```

Note that the program allows you to input any number after the question mark when you run the program. Next, it computes how many digits your number has (steps 20 to 50). Then, it tests whether your number appears as the rightmost part of its square.

We always present some data that you can use to check whether or not you typed the core program correctly into your computer. By entering the data to answer the questions posed, you can tell whether you typed the program correctly and see what happens when it is run.

1. Check your program as follows. RUN it. After the question mark, input 25 and press the return key. You should obtain a printed message explaining that 25 does appear as the rightmost part of its square, 625.
2. The numbers 44 and 321 do not appear as the rightmost parts of their squares. Check them with your program.
3. Which of these numbers do appear as the rightmost parts of their squares: 4, 6, 14, 116?

Now comes the next part, Modification Suggestions. With our suggestions, you should be able to modify the core program to solve Mad Mary's Problem. Although for Mad Mary's Problem we will tell you exactly what changes you can make, we do not do that in general. If you cannot decide what to do from the suggestions, look at the program solution in Part III, which includes all of the suggested modifications.

Modification Suggestions

☐ To discover all six numbers of less than 400 that Mad Mary used as product codes for her six plastic squares, modify the core program as follows.

1. Replace the INPUT statement with a FOR–NEXT loop so that all the values of *N* from *N* = 1 to *N* = 399 can be checked by the program. You can do this with two specific modifications:
   a) Replace line 10 with
      10 FOR N=1 to 399
   b) Add line 135
      135 NEXT N

   In this way, you build a FOR–NEXT loop around all the steps of the program that are used to test each particular value of *N*.
2. Next, change the PRINT statements so that only the six special numbers, each of which appears as the rightmost part of its square, are printed. This can be done simply by:
   a) Deleting line 100
   b) Replacing line 110 by
      110 GOTO 135

Notice that you can RUN the modified program and discover which six numbers Mad Mary used, thus solving the stated problem.

Finally, we present a selection of extensions to the original problem. Each extension is intended to be separate from the other extensions but does relate back to the original problem. The extensions are usually ordered by difficulty from easy to hard. Here we give no suggestions on how to adapt the BASIC program solution to the original problem to solve any of the extensions. You are on your own but can always consult Part V, which contains our BASIC program solutions to the extensions, or Part VI, which has the numerical answers.

Extensions

1. Suppose that Mad Mary restricted herself to choosing product codes with exactly three digits. How many plastic squares could she number using her rule?

2. If Mad Mary changes her rule and uses a product code only when it is the rightmost part of half its square, what codes of less than 1000 can she use?

3. What are all the numbers less than 100 whose cubes end in the number?

For this sample problem, the programs and numerical solutions are included in this part rather than in Parts III through VI.

BASIC PROGRAM
SOLUTION TO MAD MARY'S
PROBLEM (PART III)

```
  3 REM  MAD MARY'S PRODUCT CODES
 10 FOR N=1 TO 399
 20    FOR I=1 TO 9
 30      D=I
 40       IF N<10∧I THEN 60
 50    NEXT I
 60    S=N*N
 70    P=INT(10∧D+.5)
 80    T=S-P*INT(S/P)
 90    IF T=N THEN 120
110    GOTO 135
120    PRINT N;" IS ";
130    PRINT "THE RIGHT-MOST PART OF ";S
135 NEXT N
140 END
```

NUMERICAL ANSWERS
TO MAD MARY'S
PROBLEM (PART IV)

The numbers of the six plastic squares are 1, 5, 6, 25, 76, and 376.

BASIC PROGRAM
SOLUTION TO THE EXTENSIONS TO
MAD MARY'S PROBLEM (PART V)

```
  3 REM  MAD MARY'S PRODUCT CODES E1
 10 FOR N=100 TO 999
 20    FOR I=1 TO 9
 30      D=I
 40       IF N<10∧I THEN 60
 50    NEXT I
 60    S=N*N
 70    P=INT(10∧D+.5)
 80    T=S-P*INT(S/P)
 90    IF T=N THEN 120
110    GOTO 135
120    PRINT N;" IS ";
130    PRINT "THE RIGHT-MOST PART OF ";S
135 NEXT N
140 END
```

```
  3 REM   MAD MARY'S PRODUCT CODES E2
  8 Z=0
 10 FOR N=1 TO 999
 20    FOR I=1 TO 9
 30       D=I
 40       IF N<10^I THEN 60
 50    NEXT I
 60    S=N*N/2
 70    P=INT(10^D+.5)
 80    T=S-P*INT(S/P)
 90    IF T=N THEN 120
110    GOTO 135
120    PRINT N;" IS ";
125    Z=Z+1
130    PRINT "THE RIGHT-MOST PART OF ";S
135    IF Z=10 THEN 140
137 NEXT N
140 END
```

```
  3 REM   MAD MARY'S PRODUCT CODES E3
 10 FOR N=1 TO 99
 20    FOR I=1 TO 9
 30       D=I
 40       IF N<10^I THEN 60
 50    NEXT I
 60    S=N*N*N
 70    P=INT(10^D+.5)
 80    T=S-P*INT(S/P)
 90    IF T=N THEN 120
110    GOTO 135
120    PRINT N;" IS ";
130    PRINT "THE RIGHT-MOST PART OF ";S
135 NEXT N
140 END
```

NUMERICAL ANSWERS
TO THE EXTENSIONS
TO MAD MARY'S PROBLEM
(PART VI)

1. Mad Mary could number two squares with exactly three digits. They would be numbered 376 and 625.

2. Mad Mary could use five codes of less than 1000. They are: 2, 50, 52, 250, and 752.

3. There are 12 numbers of less than 100 whose cubes end in the number. They are: 1, 4, 5, 6, 9, 24, 25, 49, 51, 75, 76, and 99.

PROBLEMS, CORE PROGRAMS, MODIFICATION SUGGESTIONS, AND EXTENSIONS

1

Wraparound Numbers

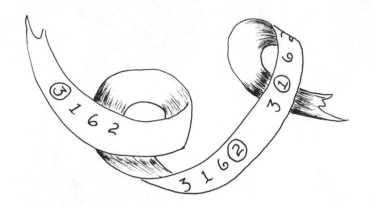

A wraparound number has three properties:

1. Each digit describes where the next one is located (by counting to the right and wrapping around when needed).
2. All the digits are landed on, once each.
3. After using each digit once, you arrive back at the original (leftmost) digit.

For example, 3162 is a wraparound number as illustrated below:

Start with the
leftmost digit, the 3 .... ③ 1 6 2

Take the number 3 and
count three digits to the
right, landing on 2 .... 3 1 6 ②

Take the number 2 and
count two digits to the
right, wrapping around to the
left, landing on 1 .... 3 ① 6 2

Take the number 1 and
count one digit to the right,
landing on 6 .... 3 1 ⑥ 2

Take the number 6 and
count six digits to the
right, wrapping around
when needed, landing on 3 .... ③ 1 6 2

Which four-digit numbers beginning with the digit 3 are wraparound numbers?

Core Program

☐ The following program will help you test whether any particular four-digit number is a wraparound number.

```
  3 REM   WRAPAROUND NUMBERS A
 10 DIM A[4]
 20 INPUT N
 30 R=N
 40 FOR I=4 TO 1 STEP -1
 50    S=INT(R/10)
 60    A[I]=R-10*S
 70    R=S
 80 NEXT I
 90 K=1
100 FOR I=1 TO 4
110    IF A[K]=0 THEN 190
120    S=K+A[K]
130    A[K]=0
140    K=S-4*INT((S-1)/4)
150 NEXT I
160 IF K<>1 THEN 190
170 PRINT "YES, ";N;" IS ";
180 GOTO 200
190 PRINT "NO, ";N;" IS NOT ";
200 PRINT "A WRAPAROUND NUMBER"
210 END
```

This program lets you input any four-digit number in line 20. It then pulls off the digits of that number one at a time and stores them in the locations A(1), A(2), A(3), and A(4). This happens in lines 30 to 80. Then in lines 90 to 160 the digits are used to test for the wraparound properties.

1. Check your program by entering 1263; you should obtain the printed message that 1263 is a wraparound number.
2. Check your program also for the number 2137, which is not a wraparound number.
3. Which of these numbers is a wraparound number: 6271 or 6543?

Modification Suggestions

☐ To modify the program in part A to find all four-digit numbers beginning with the digit 3 that are wraparound numbers, make these changes.

1. Instead of using the INPUT statement, build a FOR–NEXT loop around steps 30 to 200 in the program so that each of the values from $N = 3000$ to $N = 3999$ can be checked for the wraparound property. You can do this by replacing line 20 with FOR N = 3000 to 3999 and adding a line 205 with NEXT N.

2. Change the PRINT lines so that only the four-digit numbers that are wraparound numbers are printed. You can do this by deleting lines 180 and 200. Then replace 170 with PRINT N and 190 with GOTO 205.

Extensions

1. The twentieth-century year 1951 is a wraparound year. What are the first and last years in the twentieth century that are wraparound numbers?
2. How many four-digit wraparound numbers are there?
3. How many three-digit wraparound numbers are there?

Sums of Squares

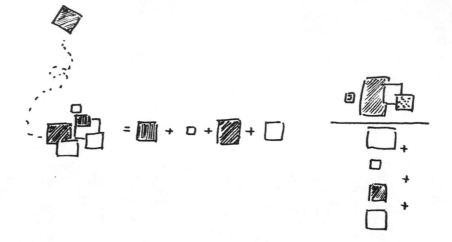

Some numbers, such as 29 and 72, are sums of two squares: $29 = 5^2 + 2^2$, $72 = 6^2 + 6^2$. Other numbers are not the sums of two squares; for example, 24 and 51.

Some numbers, however, are sums of two squares in several ways. Note that $125 = 10^2 + 5^2$ and $125 = 2^2 + 11^2$.

What whole numbers of less than 125 are the sum of two squares in *two* different ways?

Core Program

☐ Central to this problem is deciding whether a number is the sum of two squares at all. Here is a BASIC program to accomplish this task:

```
  3 REM   SUMS OF SQUARES A
 10 INPUT N
 20 PRINT "THE NUMBER  ";"FIRST SQUARE  ";"SECOND SQUARE"
 30 PRINT
 40 FOR A=1 TO INT(SQR(N))+1
 50   FOR B=1 TO A
 60     J=A*A+B*B
 70     IF J<>N THEN 90
 80     PRINT N,A,B
 90   NEXT B
100 NEXT A
110 END
```

Note that the nested FOR–NEXT loops assemble all the combinations of sums of two squares for comparison with *N*, a number of your choice. All the ways in which *N* is the sum of two squares, if any, will be printed.

1. Run this program and check the known data for the numbers 29 and 72.

2. Is 500 the sum of two squares?

3. What is special about 325?

Modification Suggestions

☐ To find the smallest whole number that is the sum of two squares in two different ways, make these changes in the program of part A.

1. Instead of using the INPUT statement, build a FOR–NEXT loop around the program so that all values of *N* between 1 and, say, 125 can be tested. Start the loop just after the PRINT statements at the beginning of the program.

2. Choose a location, say *C*, as a counter to count the number of ways that a number *N* can be written as the sum of two squares. Start the value of *C* at zero just *after* the FOR–NEXT loop that replaced the INPUT statement. Add 1 to *C* every time a new way of writing *N* as the sum of two squares is found.

3. Include an IF–THEN test to check if two ways to write *N* as the sum of two squares have been found. If not, save the current values of *A* and *B* in two locations, say A1 and B1, just before the NEXT B statement. If so, PRINT N, A, B and N, A1, B1.

Extensions

1. What is the smallest number that is the sum of two squares in three different ways? in four different ways?

2. Some numbers are the sum of two equal squares but not the sum of two unequal squares: for example, $72 = 6^2 + 6^2$. What is the smallest number that is the sum of two unequal squares in two different ways?

3. What is the smallest number that is the sum of two cubes in two different ways? of two unequal cubes in two different ways?

Double Deal

Harry Sampson, the magician, has a deck of nine cards, each with one of the numbers 1, 2, 3, 4, 5, 6, 7, 8, and 9 on it. By arranging the cards properly, Harry can deal them in such a way that when the first four cards are grouped together to form a four-digit number and the remaining five cards form a five-digit number, the larger number is exactly twice as large as the smaller one.

This is just such a deal:

$$7 \ 9 \ 2 \ 3 \qquad 1 \ 5 \ 8 \ 4 \ 6$$

There are other "double" deals like this. What is the smallest four-digit number giving a "double" deal?

Core Program

□ One way to approach a solution to this problem is to choose a four-digit number, *N*, double it, obtaining *M*, and check whether the nine digits in *N* and *M* are all the nine distinct digits from 1 to 9. The following program will accomplish this feat in a rather unusual fashion:

```
  3 REM   DOUBLE DEAL A
 10 INPUT N
 20 S=0
 30 P=1
 40 R=N
 50 GOSUB 400
 60 M=2*N
 70 R=M
 80 GOSUB 400
 90 IF S<>285 THEN 120
100 IF P<>362880 THEN 120
110 PRINT N;" ITS DOUBLE ";M;" USE ALL 9 DIGITS"
120 END
400 K=R/10
410 D=INT(10*(K-INT(K))+.5)
420 R=INT(K)
430 S=S+D*D
440 P=P*D
450 IF R<>0 THEN 400
460 RETURN
```

In this program *S* is the sum of the squares of all the digits of *N* and its double *M*. Similarly, *P* is the product of all the digits of *N* and *M*. Notice that a subroutine in lines 400 to 460 is used to pick off the single digits of *N* and *M*, as well as add the squares of those digits into *S* and multiply those digits onto *P*. Once the squared-digit sum, *S*, and digit product, *P*, are computed, the program compares them to 285 and 362,880, respectively. Here the program uses the little-known mathematical fact that any set of nine digits with those exact squared-digit sum and digit products must be the set of nine distinct digits, one through nine, with no duplicates. Thus, the program tests whether *N* and its double *M* use all nine digits 1 to 9.

1. Run this program to check that in a deal where 7923 is the four-digit number, the five-digit number formed as its double uses the rest of the nine digits.
2. Verify that in a deal where 6173 is the four-digit number, the other five digits do not form a number that is exactly twice as large.

Modification Suggestions

☐ To discover the "double" deal with the smallest four-digit number, make these changes in the program of part A.

1. Instead of using the INPUT statement, build a FOR–NEXT loop around the program to test all the possible values of N. Since the double of N needs to be a five-digit number which is at least as large as 12,345, N must be at least 6173. Furthermore, N need not be any larger than 9999.

2. Replace line 120 with the NEXT statement and follow it by an END statement.

3. Use a GOTO statement after the PRINT statement to END the program as soon as a result is obtained.

4. Immediately following the FOR statement, you could include a line 15 as follows:

$$15 \quad \text{PRINT} \quad N,$$

This will let you see the four-digit values of N as they are considered.

Extensions

1. Can you find any pair of four- and five-digit numbers using each of the digits 1 through 9 just once each, where the larger is three times the smaller? four times the smaller?

2. There is a unique pair of numbers, one with four digits and one with five, which uses the digits 1 to 9 and in which the larger is 18 times the smaller. What are the two numbers?

3. No pair of numbers exist using all the digits 1 to 9 once each, where the larger is 10 times the other or 25 times the other. For what multiples do such pairs exist?

4

Reciprocal Triples

Pythagorean triples are triples (A, B, C) of positive integers so that

$$A^2 + B^2 = C^2$$

Examples of Pythagorean triples are (5, 12, 13) and (6, 8, 10), since $5^2 + 12^2 = 13^2$ and $6^2 + 8^2 = 10^2$. The triple with the smallest sum is (3, 4, 5).

Interestingly, reciprocal Pythagorean triples exist. These are triples (A, B, C) of positive integers with the property

$$\frac{1}{A^2} + \frac{1}{B^2} = \frac{1}{C^2}$$

An example of a reciprocal Pythagorean triple is (156, 65, 60) since

$$\frac{1}{156^2} + \frac{1}{65^2} = \frac{1}{60^2}$$

What are the two reciprocal Pythagorean triples with sums of less than 100?

Core Program

☐ To tackle this question, it is instructive first to write a program to generate ordinary Pythagorean triples and their respective sums. Here is one such BASIC program:

```
  3 REM   RECIPROCAL TRIPLES A
 10 INPUT N
 20 PRINT TAB(5);"A";TAB(12);"B";TAB(19);"C";TAB(30);"A+B+C"
 30 PRINT
 40 FOR A=1 TO N
 50   FOR B=1 TO A
 60     Z=(A*A+B*B)
 70     C=INT(SQR(Z))
 80     IF C*C<>Z THEN 100
 90     PRINT TAB(5);A;TAB(12);B;TAB(19);C;TAB(30);A+B+C
100   NEXT B
110 NEXT A
120 END
```

In this program the triples are formed from the equation

$$C = \sqrt{A^2 + B^2}$$

Depending on the value of *N* selected, *A* and *B* loop from 1 to *N*. The program then produces all the Pythagorean triples in that range. By inspecting the various printed sums, you can determine by eye the triple (or triples) with the minimal sum.

Lines 70 and 80 are used to avoid possible round-off errors when the square root is calculated. Whether or not round-off errors occur depends on how your system is designed to compute a square root.

1. Check to see that the program works. For $N = 5$ there is 1 Pythagorean triple with a sum of 12.
2. Using $N = 20$, find all seven Pythagorean triples with $1 \leq A \leq 20$ and $1 \leq B \leq 20$.
3. What is the triple with the minimal sum? Note that any Pythagorean triple outside the range used will have each positive integer being at least as large as 20, so the sum of all three will be larger than 40. This observation will be enough to conclude which triple has the minimal sum without running the program for any other values of *N*.

Modification Suggestions

☐ To locate the two reciprocal Pythagorean triples with sums of less than 100, several modifications of the program in part A are needed.

1. Change line 60 so that the program generates integer triples with the reciprocal property

$$\frac{1}{A^2} + \frac{1}{B^2} = \frac{1}{C^2}$$

This can be done after solving the equation for C and obtaining

$$C = \sqrt{\frac{A^2 B^2}{A^2 + B^2}}$$

2. When a reciprocal triple is obtained, include an IF–THEN test to determine whether or not the sum, $A + B + C$, is less than 100.

3. To count the number of sums less than 100 for reciprocal triples, choose a location, say T. Set T equal to zero at the beginning of the program. Add 1 each time a reciprocal triple is printed.

4. Include a test to END the program when the two reciprocal Pythagorean triples with sums less than 100 are obtained.

5. INPUT a large value of N so that the program obtains a large number of triples. Since the triple (156, 65, 60) is already known, and the corresponding sum is 281, it will be sufficient to use $N = 281$.

Extensions

1. Consider the triples given by the equation

$$\frac{1}{A^3} + \frac{1}{B^3} = \frac{1}{C^3}$$

What is the minimal triple?

2. What is the minimal triple for the following reciprocal property?

$$\frac{1}{A} + \frac{1}{B} = \frac{1}{C}$$

3. Is there a minimal quadruple for the following equation?

$$\frac{1}{A^2} + \frac{1}{B^2} + \frac{1}{C^2} = \frac{1}{D^2}$$

Chains of
Condensed Numbers

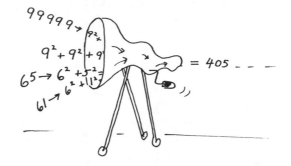

What happens if you condense a number by taking its digits, squaring them, and adding the products? Sometimes this process produces a smaller number; two examples are:

$$65 \to 6^2 + 5^2 = 36 + 25 = 61$$

$$61 \to 6^2 + 1^2 = 36 + 1 = 37$$

But, sometimes this condensation produces a larger number; for example:

$$37 \to 3^2 + 7^2 = 9 + 49 = 58$$

For very large numbers, the condensation is definitely smaller:

$$99999 \to 9^2 + 9^2 + 9^2 + 9^2 + 9^2 = (5)(81) = 405$$

If you condense a number in this fashion, condense the result, and continue condensing, you produce a chain of condensed numbers with a surprising property. All condensed number chains eventually reach a loop containing 37 or reach the number 1. Note these examples:

$$65 \to 61 \to 37 \to 58 \to 89 \to 145 \to 42 \to 20 \to 4 \to 16 \to 37 \to 58 \to \text{etc.}$$

$$400 \to 16 \to 37 \to 58 \to 89 \to 145 \to 42 \to 20 \to 4 \to 16 \to 37 \to 58 \to \text{etc.,}$$

$$\text{whereas } 44 \to 32 \to 13 \to 10 \to 1 \to 1 \to 1 \to \text{etc.}$$

Let us say that the length of a condensed number chain is the number of condensations needed to reach either the number 37 or the number 1. What are all the two-digit numbers with chains of length 14 or more?

Core Program

☐ In the process of finding the two-digit numbers with chains of length at least 14, it helps to have a program that produces the result of one condensation. Here is such a program:

```
  3 REM   CHAINS OF CONDENSED NUMBERS A
 10 INPUT N
 20 R=N
 30 C=0
 40 K=R/10
 50 D=INT(10*(K-INT(K))+.5)
 60 R=INT(K)
 70 C=C+D*D
 80 IF R<>0 THEN 40
 90 PRINT C
100 END
```

Note how the program picks off digits, *D*, of any number you choose, one at a time, and adds the square of each of those digits to a running total, *C*.

1. Try this program on $N = 65$ and $N = 99,999$ to see that you obtain 61 and 405, respectively.

2. By rerunning this program, you can verify that the number chain starting at 65 is the one given above and eventually reaches the loop with 37. Does 23 start a chain that reaches the 37 loop or a chain that ends at 1?

3. What happens to 70? to 71?

Modification Suggestions

☐ When adapting the program from part A to find all two-digit numbers that have chains of at least 14 numbers, make these changes.

1. Replace the INPUT statement with a FOR–NEXT loop to test all possible two-digit numbers.

2. Insert a GOTO statement in place of the PRINT statement in line 90 so that the program loops back to repeat the condensation process (lines 20 through 80) on each condensed number.

3. Choose a location, *X*, to keep track of the count of the length of the chain. Start *X* at a value of zero just *after* the FOR statement. Add 1 to *X* just after line 80 when the program completes a condensation process.

4. Immediately following the addition of 1 to the counter established in step 3, insert IF–THEN tests to see whether or not the condensed number has reached 37 or 1. If not, rename the current value of *C* as *R* and loop back to repeat the condensation process as set up in step 2. If the condensed number is either 37 or 1, proceed to step 5.

5. Insert an IF–THEN test just after the GOTO statement to decide if a particular chain has a length of at least 14. When *X* shows a chain length of 14 or more, PRINT N, X, and C.

Extensions

1. What is the longest chain for a two-digit number? a three-digit number? a four-digit number?

2. What are all the two-digit numbers whose condensed number chains end at 1?

3. How many three-digit numbers have chains of length 15 or more?

6

What's the Odometer Read?

Laurie was driving from her home to Maine in her 12-year-old car. To keep track of the number of miles driven, she set the trip odometer to zero (see Figure 1).

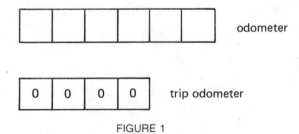

FIGURE 1

At the end of her trip, Laurie had traveled a total of X miles. She noticed that the number of miles on the trip odometer was the same as the number formed by the last three digits on the odometer. Furthermore, the number on the odometer was exactly the square of the number of miles on the trip odometer.

How many miles did Laurie travel?

Core Program

☐ To solve this problem it is helpful to have a program that picks off the three rightmost digits of the square of a three-digit number. Here is such a program:

```
 3 REM  WHAT'S THE ODOMETER READ? A
10 INPUT X
20 Y=X*X-INT(X*X/1000)*1000
30 PRINT X,X*Y,Y
40 END
```

Note that for any number X, $X \times X$ is the square of X, and Y is the rightmost three digits of $X \times X$.

1. Check the program by inputting 112 for X. Since $112 \times 112 = 12,544$, you should find that $Y = 544$.
2. Does the program work for $X = 100$?
3. What are the three rightmost digits for 999^2?

Modification Suggestions

☐ To find out how many miles Laurie traveled, make these changes in the program in part A.

1. Using an IF–THEN test, determine if $X = Y$. If it does, PRINT Y.

2. Instead of using the INPUT X statement, build a FOR–NEXT loop around the program to check all three-digit values of X from 100 to 999.

Extensions

1. On a trip in her brother's car, Laurie noticed that the square of the number of miles on the trip odometer equaled the number on the odometer. But the number formed by the last three digits on the odometer was twice the number on the trip odometer. What number was on the trip odometer?

2. What numbers would appear on the trip odometer if the last three digits on the odometer were three, four, or five times the number on the trip odometer? Of course, the square of the number on the trip odometer equals the number on the odometer.

3. Is there a three-digit number N such that the number formed by any three consecutive digits of N^2 equals N?

Zip Codes

One day a mail sorter saw a letter addressed and stamped as shown in Figure 2.

Postage Due 12¢

P. O. Box 1936
Richmond, VA 23232

FIGURE 2

The sorter, an amateur mathematician, found the letter most unusual. It caught his eye since the box number was the same as the year of his birth, 1936.

As he looked at the letter he noticed that the five-digit zip code was a *palindrome*—a number reading the same right to left and left to right. The sum of the palindrome's digits happened to be 12, the amount of the postage due. Of even greater interest, when the zip code was divided by the sum of its digits the result was 1936!

The sorter wondered if the year of his birth equaled any other five-digit palindromes divided by the sum of their digits. Are there others?

Core Program

☐ To solve this problem it is helpful to have a program that outputs five-digit palindromes. Here is such a program:

```
3 REM  ZIP CODES A
10 FOR A=1 TO 9
20    FOR B=0 TO 9
30       FOR C=0 TO 9
40          P=(10*A+B)*1000+(C*100)+(10*B+A)
50          PRINT P,
60       NEXT C
70    NEXT B
80 NEXT A
90 END
```

Note that the computation of P produces the palindrome *ABCBA* in the form $(10 \times A + B) \times 1000 + (C \times 100) + (10 \times B + A)$, which equals $A \times 10{,}000 + B \times 1000 + C \times 100 + B \times 10 + A$.

Run the program to see if you entered it correctly. The output will be the 900 five-digit palindromes, the last five of which are 99,599, 99,699, 99,799, 99,899, and 99,999.

Modification Suggestions

☐ To find which five-digit palindromes divided by the sums of their digits equal 1936, make two modifications in the program of part A.

1. Compute the sum of the digits of each palindrome as $2 \times A + 2 \times B + C$ (or $A + B + C + B + A$)

2. Use an IF–THEN test to determine when the palindrome divided by the sum of its digits equals 1936. When it is, PRINT the palindrome, the sum, and the result of the division.

Extensions

1. There are a total of 112 five-digit palindromes that yield a whole number when divided by the sums of their digits. What is the smallest? the largest?

2. There are six five-digit palindromes that yield a whole number when divided by the sums of their digits such that all the digits except one are identical: for example, 55,755. What are the other five?

3. There are 11 four-digit palindromes that yield a whole number when divided by the sums of their digits. But only one of them has a whole number greater than 400. What is it?

8

Temperature Teaser

One of the coldest days of the year saw the temperature (Fahrenheit) fall to 40 degrees below zero. On the news, which gives the temperature in both Fahrenheit and Celsius, the announcer stated with amazement that the Celsius temperature was also 40 degrees below zero.

There are exactly two other Fahrenheit temperatures for which the Celsius temperature is the same. What are they?

Core Program

☐ To solve this problem it is useful to have a program that converts temperatures from Fahrenheit to Celsius. Here is such a program:

```
 3 REM  TEMPERATURE TEASER A
10 INPUT F
20 C=5/9*(F-32)
30 IF (C-INT(C))*10>=5 THEN 60
40 C1=INT(C)
50 GOTO 70
60 C1=INT(C)+1
70 PRINT "C=";C1
80 END
```

An important feature in the program reflects the fact that temperatures are reported as whole numbers. Thus, the program, which converts Fahrenheit to Celsius by the formula $C = 5/9 \times (F - 32)$, rounds C to the nearest whole number (see line 30).

1. Check the program for $F = 32$. You should obtain $C = 0$.
2. What do you obtain for $F = 212$?
3. Does the program work for negative values of F?

Modification Suggestions

☐ To find the two other Fahrenheit temperatures for which the Celsius temperatures are the same, make these changes in the program in part A.

1. Replace the PRINT statement with an IF–THEN test to determine if $F = C$. When they are equal, PRINT F and C.
2. Instead of using the INPUT statement, build a FOR–NEXT loop around the program and test all values of F between -100 and 100.

Extensions

1. A temperature of 186 degrees Fahrenheit is 86 degrees Celsius. For what other Fahrenheit temperatures does dropping the hundreds digit give the Celsius temperature?

2. A temperature of 61 degrees Fahrenheit is 16 degrees Celsius. The Celsius temperature is the reverse of the Fahrenheit temperature. Are there any others?

3. A temperature of 104 degrees Fahrenheit is 40 degrees Celsius. For what other Fahrenheit temperatures does dropping the hundreds digit and reversing the remaining digits give the Celsius temperature?

9

Multiply Perfect Numbers

When the sum of the divisions of an integer n is a multiple of n, we call n a *multiply perfect number*. For example, 28 is a multiply perfect number since the sum of its divisors is twice the number: that is,

$$1 + 2 + 4 + 7 + 14 + 28 = 56 = 2 \times 28$$

What are all multiply perfect numbers of less than 1000?

Core Program

☐ To find all multiply perfect numbers of less than 1000, it is helpful to have a program to find all the divisors of any particular number.

```
  3 REM  MULTIPLY PERFECT NUMBERS A
 10 INPUT N
 20 Q=SQR(N)
 30 FOR D1=1 TO Q
 40    D2=N/D1
 50    IF D2<>INT(D2) THEN 90
 60    IF D2=D1 THEN 80
 70    PRINT D2,
 80    PRINT D1,
 90 NEXT D1
100 END
```

Note that Q is the name for the square root of N, D1 is a possible first divisor of N, and D2 is a possible second divisor of N. D1 will be a divisor only when D2 is an integer. D2 is then also a divisor.

1. Check this program for $N = 12$ and $N = 16$; you should see that 12 has the six divisors 1, 2, 3, 4, 6, and 12, while 16 has the five divisors 1, 2, 4, 8, and 16.

2. How many divisors does 24 have?

3. What is the sum of the divisors of 20?

Modification Suggestions

☐ To find all multiply perfect numbers between 1 and 1000, make these changes in the program in part A.

1. Choose a location, say *S*, to hold the sum of the divisors of *N*. Start *S* with a value of zero. Then instead of printing each divisor of *N*, add that divisor to *S*.

2. Include an IF–THEN statement to test whether *S* is a multiple of *N*, and if so, PRINT out the values of *N* and *S*.

3. Instead of using the INPUT statement, build a FOR–NEXT loop around the program so that all values of *N* between 1 and 1000 can be tested.

Extensions

1. What is the smallest odd integer (less than 1000) for which the sum of its divisors is larger than twice the number? This number is called the *smallest odd abundant number*.

2. The number 24 has eight divisors and 8 divides evenly into 24. For what other integers between 1 and 100 does the number of divisors (rather than the sum of the divisors) divide evenly into the number?

3. What integers between 1 and 100 have an odd number of divisors?

10

Locker Numbers

One day Beth remarked to Bob that her school locker number added to 100 times his locker number equaled the student enrollment at the school. Bob pointed out that the product of their different locker numbers also equaled the student enrollment at the school.

If the number of students at the school was between 1000 and 10,000 and was a perfect square, what were Beth and Bob's locker numbers?

Core Program

☐ To solve this problem it is helpful to have a program giving integer values satisfying the equation $X + 100Y = XY$, where X is Beth's locker number and Y is Bob's locker number. Here is such a program:

```
 3 REM  LOCKER NUMBERS A
10 INPUT Y
20 PRINT
30 PRINT "X","Y","X*Y"
40 PRINT
50 X=100*Y/(Y-1)
60 PRINT X,Y,X*Y
70 END
```

This program uses the fact in step 50 that the equation $X + 100Y = XY$ can be solved for X as follows:

$$X + 100Y = XY$$

$$100Y = XY - X$$

$$100Y = X(Y - 1)$$

$$\frac{100Y}{(Y - 1)} = X$$

1. Check your program by entering 9 for Y; you should then get $X = 112.5$ and $X \times Y = 1012.5$.
2. Does $Y = 6$ produce an integer value for X?
3. For $Y = 5$, is the corresponding $X \times Y$ a perfect square? Why doesn't this value produce a solution to the locker problem?

Modification Suggestions

☐ To modify the program in part A to find integers X and Y whose product is a perfect square and between 1000 and 10,000, make these changes.

1. Insert an IF–THEN test to decide whether X is a whole number.

2. Insert an IF–THEN test to decide whether $X \times Y$ is a perfect square. This can be a tricky test on your home computer, since round-off errors creep into the calculations of square roots and exponentiation. For example, these statements may fail to notice that $X \times Y$ is a perfect square when it really is one:

sample step 25 IF X*Y < > INT(SQR(X*Y)) ∧ 2 THEN 60

or 25 IF INT(SQR(X*Y)) < > SQR(X*Y) THEN 60

Instead, you will likely have more success with this pair of basic statements:

24 Z = INT(SQR(X*Y))

26 IF X*Y < > Z*Z THEN 60

3. Insert IF–THEN tests to decide whether $X \times Y$ is between 1000 and 10,000.

4. Also, instead of using an INPUT statement to test specific Y values, build a FOR–NEXT loop around the program to test lots of Y values. Place the FOR statement just after the PRINT statements at the beginning of the program.

Extensions

1. Bill's locker number added to 110 times Jill's locker number equals the product of their locker numbers. If the sum of their locker numbers is 222, what is each of their locker numbers?

2. There exist many integer triples X, Y, Z such that $X + 10Y + 100Z = XYZ$. For what values of X, Y, Z is the product XYZ minus 5 a perfect square?

3. What three consecutive integers X, Y, Z satisfy the relationship $X + 10Y + 100Z = XYZ$?

11

Age Arrangements

Sarah Hatfield, a 29-year-old waitress, happened to write the ages of her three children next to one another. Interestingly, she noticed that the three-digit number formed, divided by the sum of the children's ages, equaled her own age. What were the ages of her three children, and what three-digit number did they form?

Core Program

☐ Using one approach to solving this problem involves the idea of how to form a three-digit number given each of the digits.

```
 3 REM   AGE ARRANGEMENTS A
10 FOR X=1 TO 9
20   FOR Y=0 TO 9
30     FOR Z=0 TO 9
40       N=100*X+10*Y+Z
50         PRINT N
60       NEXT Z
70     NEXT Y
80 NEXT X
90 END
```

Running this program you will see in sequence all three-digit numbers from 100 to 999.

The variables X, Y, and Z represent the hundreds, tens, and units digits, respectively, for each three-digit number N. Line 40 of the program forms the three-digit number as $100X + 10Y + Z$.

Modification Suggestions

☐ To adapt the program from part A to find the solution to Sarah Hatfield's age question, make these changes.

1. Compute the sum of the three children's ages.

2. Then include an IF–THEN test to decide whether the three-digit number N, when divided by the sum of the children's ages, gives 28.

Extensions

1. Sarah's boss, 81-year-old Willie Newman, has four grand-children. When their ages are written next to one another, a four-digit number is formed. Dividing the four-digit number by the sum of the ages of the grandchildren equals Willie's age. What are the grandchildren's ages, and what four-digit number do they form?

2. Sarah's brother Henry is 43. He has two teenage children. Their ages written next to each other form a four-digit number. Dividing the four-digit number by the sum of the ages of the teenagers equals Henry's age. What are the ages of the teen-agers, and what four-digit number do they form?

3. Fourteen-year-old Beth has three cousins under the age of 25. If the ages of her cousins are written next to one another, with the youngest listed last, a five-digit number is formed. Dividing the five-digit number by the product of the ages of the cousins equals Beth's age. What are the ages of the cousins, and what five-digit number do they form?

The Multiplier Effect

Henry walked into math class one day and saw this problem on the board:

multiplicand	multiplier	product
2178	× 4 =	8712

The class was working on multiplication problems involving four-digit multiplicands and one-digit multipliers. Henry noticed that the digits in the multiplicand, 2178, reversed gave the correct product 8712. He asked the teacher if any other four-digit by one-digit multiplication problems had the same unusual property. The teacher replied that there are many obvious examples for the multiplier 1 (such as 3333 × 1 = 3333) but only one other example when the single-digit multiplier was greater than 1.

What was the multiplier and the corresponding four-digit multiplicand?

Core Program

☐ To find the other multiplier and multiplicand, it helps to have a program that reverses the digits of any number. Here is such a program:

```
  3 REM   THE MULTIPLIER EFFECT A
 10 INPUT N
 20 R=0
 30 P=N
 40 K=P/10
 50 P=INT(K)
 60 D=INT(10*(K-P)+.5)
 70 R=10*R+D
 80 IF P<>0 THEN 40
 90 PRINT R
100 END
```

Note that steps 40 to 80 of the program form a loop which picks off the digits, *D*, of *N* one at a time and forms the reverse *R* of the number.

1. Try the program with an input of 1234. You should get the reverse 4321 as an output.

2. Find the reverses of 234, 2345, 23,456, and 234,567.

3. What happens when you have the program reverse the number 24,680?

Modification Suggestions

☐ Make these changes to the program in part A so that the program can find the multiplier and multiplicand that the teacher was thinking about.

1. Insert an IF–THEN test to check whether dividing the number *N* into its reverse *R* gives a whole number.

2. Insert other IF–THEN tests to eliminate the cases where *R* and *N* are equal and where $N = 2178$.

3. Instead of using the INPUT statement, build a FOR–NEXT loop around the program so that the program checks all four-digit integers.

4. Replace the PRINT statement so that the multiplicand, *N*, the multiplier, $\frac{R}{N}$, and the product, *R*, are displayed. Since there is only one solution, use a GOTO statement after printing the results to END the program.

Extensions

1. The multiplier effect also works for some five-digit numbers. For example, 10,989 × 9 = 98,901. Can you find another five-digit example that has a multiplier greater than 1?

2. The example in extension 1 is most interesting. The product, 98,901, is indeed the reverse of the multiplicand, 10,989. However, the product is also related to the multiplicand in another way. Think of the digits of the multiplicand as being represented by *abcde*. Then the product is equal to the last three digits of the multiplicand, *cde*, followed by the first two digits, *ab*, reversed. Thus, the product is *cdeab*. For multipliers greater than 1, there are two other examples satisfying this condition. One of them is 23,958 × 4 = 95,832. Find the other.

3. Let *a*, *b*, *c*, *d*, and *e* be digits where *abcd* is a four-digit multiplicand and *e* is a one-digit multiplier greater than 1. Find all examples such that *abcd* × *e* = *cdba*.

13

Reverse and Add

Palindromes are numbers that read the same from left to right and right to left (e.g., 11, 929, 1001, 12,321, etc.).

Take any two-digit number between 10 and 88, reverse it, and add. If the sum is not a palindrome, reverse the sum and add. Continue the process until a palindrome is reached. Several examples are shown.

$$
\begin{array}{r}
23 \\
+\ 32 \\
\hline
55
\end{array}
\qquad
\begin{array}{r}
48 \\
+\ 84 \\
\hline
132 \\
+\ 231 \\
\hline
363
\end{array}
\qquad
\begin{array}{r}
68 \\
+\ 86 \\
\hline
154 \\
+\ 451 \\
\hline
605 \\
+\ 506 \\
\hline
1111
\end{array}
$$

The numbers 23, 48, and 68 produce palindromes after one, two and three additions, respectively.

One of the integers between 10 and 88 requires six additions. Which integer is it?

Core Program

☐ To explore this problem it is useful to have a procedure to reverse a number. Here is a program to do so:

```
  3 REM   REVERSE AND ADD A
 10 INPUT N
 20 S=N
 30 Y=INT(LOG(S)/LOG(10))+1
 40 X=0
 50 R=S
 60 FOR A=1 TO Y
 70   K=R/10
 80   R=INT(K)
 90   D=INT(10*(K-R)+.5)
100   X=10*X+D
110 NEXT A
120 PRINT N,X
130 END
```

In line 30 the number of digits in *N* is computed and stored in *Y*. Lines 40 through 110 form *X*, the reverse of the number *N*.

1. Check the program by entering 23 as the input. You should see both 23 and its reverse 32.
2. Your program should work on 451, 2058, and 707,777. Does it?
3. Try your program with the palindrome 12,321 as the input. What do you notice?

Modification Suggestions

☐ To find out which integer between 10 and 88 requires six additions, modify the program in part A as follows.

1. Include an IF–THEN test to decide whether the number is a palindrome. This can be done by testing whether the current value of N represented by S in the program equals its reverse, X, after the reverse is formed. If the number is not a palindrome, add the number, S, to its reverse, X; store the sum in S; and loop back to the beginning of the program using a GOTO statement. If, on the other hand, the number is a palindrome, PRINT the result.

2. In order to count the number of additions required, choose a location, say C, to keep track of how many additions are done. Set the counter, C, to zero immediately following the INPUT statement at the beginning of the program. Then add 1 to C just after each addition.

3. Instead of printing the result all the time, include an IF–THEN statement to PRINT the palindrome only if the counter equals 6.

4. Finally, replace the INPUT statement with a FOR–NEXT loop so that the program will check all values of N between 10 and 88.

Extensions

1. Does the process of reversing and adding produce a palindrome for *all* two-digit numbers?
2. What is the smallest number requiring two additions to produce a palindrome? three additions? four additions?
3. Does the process of reversing and adding always produce a palindrome that is a multiple of 11?

14

Different Digits

During a lesson on combinations, Sam's teacher stated that there are exactly 648 three-digit integers with no repeated digits. While the teacher rambled on, Sam played around with the number 648. He added its digits, squared the sum, and divided that sum into 648. He was pleased to find no remainder.

Of all the other three-digit numbers with no repeating digits, how many have no remainder when divided by the square of the sum of the digits? What are they?

Core Program

☐ To solve this problem it helps to have a program that generates all the three-digit numbers with no repeated digits. Here is one such program:

```
  3 REM   DIFFERENT DIGITS A
 10 FOR A=1 TO 9
 20    FOR B=0 TO 9
 30       FOR C=0 TO 9
 40          IF (A-B)*(B-C)*(A-C)=0 THEN 70
 50          N=100*A+10*B+C
 60          PRINT N,
 70       NEXT C
 80    NEXT B
 90 NEXT A
100 END
```

Note how the number *ABC* is formed in line 50. Note also that the product $(A - B) \times (B - C) \times (A - C)$ will be zero only if at least one of the pairs of digits of the number *ABC* are equal.

When you run the program you will see all 648 three-digit numbers with no repeated digits, the last six of which are 982, 983, 984, 985, 986, and 987.

Modification Suggestions

☐ To adapt the program from part A to find each three-digit number with no repeating digits for which the number is a multiple of the square of the sum of its digits, make these changes:

1. Include in the program a line to compute the square of the sum of the digits of each one of the three-digit numbers formed.

2. Include an IF–THEN test to check whether the number divided by the square of the sum of its digits is a whole number and if so, PRINT the result.

3. To count the total of the numbers found and printed, choose a location, say *T*, to tally this number. At the very beginning of the program, set the counter *T* to zero. Just after printing each number found, add one to *T*. Then at the end of the program, PRINT the value of *T*.

Extensions

1. How many three-digit numbers *with* repeated digits also have the property that each divided by the square of the sum of its digits gives no remainder? What are they?
2. How many four-digit numbers are there that have no repeated digits?
3. Of all the four-digit numbers with no repeated digits, how many give no remainder when divided by the square of the sum of the digits? What is the smallest? What is the largest?

15

Positive Differences

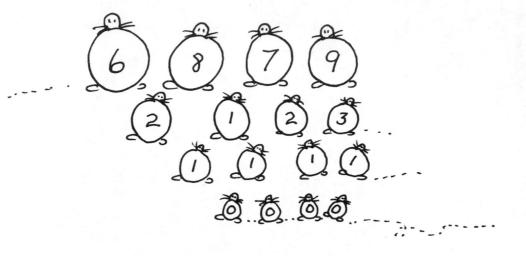

Choose any four digits. Take the positive difference between the first and second, between the second and third, between the third and fourth, and between the fourth and first digits.

For example, starting with the digits

6, 8, 7, 9

the positive differences are

2, 1, 2, 3

If you repeat the process of taking positive differences, those differences become smaller and smaller and soon reach zero.

From   2, 1, 2, 3

you get 1, 1, 1, 1

and   0, 0, 0, 0

What sets of four digits, no digit of which is bigger than 4, require repeating the process of taking positive differences seven times before reaching 0, 0, 0, 0?

Core Program

☐ To solve this problem, here is a program that takes a set of four digits and finds the first set of positive differences:

```
  3 REM   POSITIVE DIFFERENCES A
 10 PRINT "INPUT FOUR NUMBERS SEPARATED BY COMMAS"
 20 INPUT A,B,C,D
 30 GOSUB 400
 40 E=A
 50 A=ABS(A-B)
 60 B=ABS(B-C)
 70 C=ABS(C-D)
 80 D=ABS(D-E)
 90 GOSUB 400
100 END
400 PRINT A
410 PRINT TAB(9);B
420 PRINT TAB(17);C
430 PRINT TAB(25);D
440 RETURN
```

Note how the printing is done in a subroutine with GOSUB and RETURN statements.

1. Enter the digits 6, 8, 7, 9 and check that the first set of positive differences is 2, 1, 2, 3.

2. What are the first sets of positive differences when you begin with 9, 8, 7, 6? with 2, 3, 4, 5? with 5, 6, 7, 8?

3. What set of four digits gives 8, 8, 8, 8 as its first set of differences?

Modification Suggestions

☐ To adapt the program in part A to find all the sets of four digits, none bigger than 4, which require taking positive differences seven times before reaching 0, 0, 0, 0, make these changes.

1. Include an IF–THEN test after the new set of four differences is printed to check whether all of those differences are zero. Checking whether the sum of all four digits totals zero does the job. If the sum is not zero, loop back to line 40.

2. Include a counter, T, to keep track of how many times a new set of positive differences is formed. Just after the INPUT statement set the counter T to zero. Then after completing the computations for each new set of differences, add 1 to the counter.

3. Replace the INPUT statement by four FOR–NEXT loops so that the program will automatically check all the possible sets of input values for A, B, C, and D. *Caution:* If you use A, B, C, and D for the labels in the FOR and NEXT statements, the program will get caught in an infinite loop. This is because those values are the positive differences and keep getting changed back to zero. To correct this problem, have the FOR–NEXT loops use four new labels, say I, J, K, and L. Then copy the values of I, J, K, and L into the locations A, B, C, and D.

4. Finally, delete lines 30 and 90 so that all the sets of differences will not be printed. (You do not need to delete the subroutine; it may be useful when solving the extensions.)

5. Include an IF–THEN test to PRINT the original set I, J, K, L only if it takes eight loops before reaching 0, 0, 0, 0.

Extensions

1. Find a set of four digits that requires eight repetitions of the process of taking positive differences before reaching 0, 0, 0, 0.

2. How many repetitions are required if the set of four numbers is not restricted to single digits, and the second, third, and fourth numbers are two times, three times, and four times as large as the first, respectively?

3. How many repetitions are required if each succeeding number in the set of four numbers is three more than the preceding number?

16

How Many Jelly Beans?

At the Harrison High School carnival, the senior class is sponsoring a contest to guess the number of jelly beans in a jar. The number of beans in the jar is less than 10,000 and when divided by 7 leaves a remainder of 1, when divided by 9 leaves a remainder of 2, and when divided by 11 leaves a remainder of 5. Furthermore, when 56 is subtracted from the number, the result is a perfect square. How many jelly beans are there?

Core Program

☐ To solve this problem it is helpful to have a program giving all numbers of less than 10,000 that leave remainders of 1, 2, and 5 when divided by 7, 9, and 11, respectively. Here is such a program:

```
 3 REM  HOW MANY JELLY BEANS? A
10 PRINT "INPUT A NUMBER";
20 INPUT X
30 IF X-7*INT(X/7)<>1 THEN 70
40 IF X-9*INT(X/9)<>2 THEN 70
50 IF X-11*INT(X/11)<>5 THEN 70
60 PRINT "YES, ";X;" HAS THE CORRECT REMAINDERS"
70 END
```

1. Try the program with 1919, which has the correct remainders.

2. Does 4123 have the correct remainders?

3. What happens with 2612 and 1226?

Modification Suggestions

☐ Make these changes to adapt the program in part A so that it will find the desired number:

1. Include an IF–THEN test to decide if the difference X minus 56 is a perfect square. Because of round-off errors inherent in the calculations of square roots and powers, you may find it unsuccessful to use an IF–THEN statement such as the following:

   55 IF INT(SQR(X−56)) < > SQR(X−56) THEN 70

You may find this combination better:

   55 Z = INT(SQR(X−56))

   56 IF (X−56) < > Z*Z THEN 70

2. Replace the INPUT statement with a FOR–NEXT loop so that the program checks all of the values between 1 and 10,000.
3. PRINT the value of X when the correct solution is found.

Extensions

1. What is the maximum number of beans less than 10,000 that would be in the jar if the number divided by 5, 7, and 9 leaves remainders of 4, 5, and 6, respectively?

2. Maxwell Smith, born in the twentieth century, had a grandson, and the differences in their ages was 60. Interestingly, both Maxwell's year of birth and his grandson's year of birth give remainders of 1, 2, 3, and 4 when divided by 3, 4, 5, and 6, respectively. When were Maxwell and his grandson born?

3. Here are several sets of divisors and corresponding remainders. Which of the sets have no numbers of less than 10,000 satisfying the condition?

	Divisors	**Corresponding remainders**
Set a	3, 5, 7, 9	1, 2, 3, 4
Set b	6, 7, 8, 9	1, 2, 3, 4
Set c	3, 5, 8, 10	1, 2, 3, 4
Set d	3, 5, 7, 9	2, 4, 6, 8

Notes

17

Arranging Soldiers in Squares

Pretend that you are the author of a mathematical puzzle book and have thought of the following type of puzzle.

A number of soldiers stand at attention in a huge square arrangement with their leader in one of the corners. Then they regroup and begin marching in N smaller squares with their leader out in front. How many soldiers are marching?

You need to choose a value of N that will make the puzzle interesting to solve. If you choose $N = 6$, your readers will have too easy a time discovering that 24 soldiers are marching.

What is the smallest value of N that you could choose and have the number of soldiers be more than 100,000?

Core Program

☐ The following program will help solve the problem, as it will find the smallest number of soldiers possible for a specific choice of *N*:

```
3 REM   ARRANGING SOLDIERS A
10 INPUT N
20 FOR Y=1 TO 3000
30    X=INT(SQR(N*Y*Y+1))
40    IF X*X=N*Y*Y+1 THEN 60
50 NEXT Y
60 PRINT N*Y*Y;" SOLDIERS"
70 END
```

This program assumes that the number of soldiers marching in *N* squares is $N \times Y \times Y$. Since these soldiers plus their leader form a square, $N \times Y \times Y + 1$ must equal a perfect square.

1. Try this program with an input of *N* = 6. You should get 24 soldiers as the output. Note, too, that 24 + 1 is a perfect square.
2. What do you get with the input *N* = 7?
3. Do you get more than 100,000 soldiers when *N* = 50?
4. What happens when *N* = 4? Actually, there is no solution when *N* itself is a square. Because the program is not designed carefully enough, your computer may produce a large, incorrect answer for the number of soldiers. When N is a perfect square, the program should indicate that there is no possible solution.

Modification Suggestions

☐ To adapt the program from part A to find the smallest value of *N* for which there are at least 100,000 soldiers, make these changes.

1. Replace the INPUT statement with a FOR–NEXT loop to allow the program to check values of *N* between 1 and 200.

2. Include just after the FOR *N* = 1 TO 200 statement an IF–THEN statement to test whether *N* itself is a perfect square. If *N* is a square, GOTO the NEXT *N*.

3. Change the PRINT statement so that the value of *N* as well as the number of soldiers is printed.

4. After the PRINT statement and before the NEXT *N* statement, include an IF–WHEN test to end the search when the number of soldiers exceeds 100,000.

Extensions

1. What is the smallest value of N for which the number of soldiers is larger than 1 million?
2. For what values of N does the number of soldiers equal N?
3. When $Y = 2$, what are the first five values of N?

The Decade
of the 1980s

In the following multiplication problem the digits of the year 1984 are written as shown. The asterisks represent other digits.

```
   1*
   9*
   8*
 **4
————
****
```

Finding the digits to replace the asterisks is not very difficult. Discovering which years in the decade of the 1980s lead to solutions and which do not is a greater challenge. How many solutions are there to this multiplication problem in the decade of the 1980s?

Core Program

☐ To help solve the problem, here is a program that finds the digits to replace the asterisks:

```
  3 REM   THE DECADE OF THE 1980'S A
 10 PRINT "INPUT THE YEAR'S DIGITS SEPARATED BY COMMAS";
 20 INPUT A,B,C,D
 30 FOR E=0 TO 9
 40   FOR F=0 TO 9
 50      G=10*A+E
 60      H=10*B+F
 70      P=G*F
 80      Q=G*B
 90      IF Q<100 THEN 200
100      IF INT(P/10)<>C THEN 200
110      IF Q-10*INT(Q/10)<>D THEN 200
120      PRINT
130      PRINT TAB(6);G
140      PRINT TAB(6);H
150      PRINT TAB(5);"---"
160      PRINT TAB(6);P
170      PRINT TAB(4);Q
180      PRINT TAB(4);"---"
190      PRINT TAB(4);G*H
200   NEXT F
210 NEXT E
220 END
```

In this program *G* and *H* are the two numbers being multiplied; *P* and *Q* are the partial products. The IF–THEN test immediately following the computation of *Q* eliminates cases where a correct multiplication occurs but the result has three digits rather than four.

1. Try the program with input 1, 9, 8, 4. You should see

```
      16
      95
      ---
      80
     144
     -------
     1520
```

2. How many solutions are there for the input year 1852?

3. How many solutions are there for the input year 1923?

Modification Suggestions

☐ To modify the program in part A to be able to find the number of years in the decade of the 1980s that have solutions, make these changes.

1. Replace line 10 with statements that set *A* to 1, *B* to 9, and *C* to 8.

2. Replace the INPUT statement with a FOR–NEXT loop so that the program tests all values of *D* between 0 and 9.

3. To count the number of solutions obtained from years in the decade, choose a location, say *T*, to keep track of that count. At the very beginning of the program set *T* to zero. Just after each solution is printed, add one to the counter. Then at the end of the program PRINT the total number of solutions, *T*.

4. Since the problem asks only for the number of years, include a GOTO statement to skip the PRINT statements in lines 120 to 190. Do not delete these lines, as you may want to use them in exploring the extensions.

Extensions

1. How many years in the twentieth century lead to solutions of the multiplication problem?

2. Is there a year in the twentieth century for which the number in the final product of the multiplication problem is a perfect square? a perfect cube? one less than a perfect square? one less than a perfect cube?

3. What years in the twentieth century lead to solutions of this similar multiplication problem?

$$
\begin{array}{r}
1* \\
9* \\
\hline
8* \\
*4 \\
\hline
**** \\
\end{array}
$$

Square Differences

Mandy the saleswoman sells mosaic tiles and always keeps meticulous records of her inventory. At the start of the day she had a number of mauve, maize, and magenta tiles, in fact a different square number of each. After recording the day's sales, she noticed that her customers had purchased a square number of each kind of tile, leaving her with an equal number of each color.

What is the fewest number of mauve, maize, and magenta tiles that Mandy could have at the end of the day?

Core Program

⊔ To find the number of tiles of each color that Mandy had at day's end, it is helpful to find all the ways that a number can be written as the difference of two squares. Here is such a program:

```
 3 REM  SQUARE DIFFERENCES A
10 INPUT N
20 FOR Y=0 TO N
30    X=INT(SQR(N+Y*Y)+.5)
40    IF X*X<>N+Y*Y THEN 60
50    PRINT X;"*";X;"-";Y;"*";Y;"=";N
60 NEXT Y
70 END
```

1. To check that you entered the program correctly, input 7. You should obtain 4*4 − 3*3 = 7.

2. Just one of the numbers 12, 17, and 22 cannot be written as the difference of two squares. Which is it?

3. Some numbers can be written as the difference of two squares in more than one way. Try the numbers 35, 88, and 117.

Modification Suggestions

☐ Since the number of tiles that Mandy has at the end of the day is the smallest number that can be written as the difference of two squares in three ways, modify the program in part A as follows:

1. To keep track of how many ways a number can be written as the difference of two squares, add a counter. Choose a location, say C, and set it equal to zero immediately after the IN-PUT statement. After the PRINT statement, add 1 to C.

2. Replace the INPUT statement with a FOR–NEXT loop to check all the numbers between 1 and some large number, say 999.

3. Insert an IF–THEN test to check whether or not three ways have been found to express N as the difference of two squares. If so, skip out of the FOR–NEXT loops and PRINT the value of N.

Extensions

1. What is the smallest number that can be written as the difference of two squares in four ways?
2. Which odd numbers between 1 and 100 can be written as the difference of two squares in only one way?
3. What are all the numbers less than 100 that can be written as the difference of two cubes?

20

Invertible Numbers

Sam went to the local deli and had to take a number and wait in line. His number was 809. When fiddling with the card, he turned it upside down and saw the number 608. "Odd," he thought, "the number 809 is invertible." He called it invertible since rotating that card 180° produced a recognizable number.

The deli's card machine issued cards with three-digit numbers between 000 and 999. How many of the numbers were invertible?

Core Program

☐ To find how many three-digit invertible numbers exist, it is helpful to have a program to determine when a number is invertible. Here is a program that shows a number and its inversion when one exists:

```
  3 REM   INVERTIBLE NUMBERS A
 10 INPUT A$
 20 B$=""
 30 L=LEN(A$)
 40 FOR J=L TO 1 STEP -1
 50    D$=MID$(A$,J,1)
 60    IF D$<>"6" AND D$<>"9" THEN 120
 70    IF D$="6" THEN 100
 80    D$="6"
 90    GOTO 130
100    D$="9"
110    GOTO 130
120    IF D$<>"8" AND D$<>"0" THEN 170
130    B$=B$+D$
140 NEXT J
150 PRINT A$;" INVERTS TO ";B$
160 GOTO 180
170 PRINT A$;" IS NOT INVERTIBLE"
180 END
```

In this program the input number is stored in A$ as a string of characters rather than as a numerical value. Line 30 calculates *L*, the length of A$, as the number of characters in the string. Line 50 takes each character in the string A$, starting with the character in the rightmost position, and places it in D$. Then D$ is tested to see if it is either 6 or 9. If so, D$ is changed to 9 or 6, respectively.

If D$ is either 8 or 0, it remains unchanged. In the case that D$ is not 6, 9, 8, or 0, the program ends with the message that the original number is not invertible. Notice that in line 130 the inverted version of the number is formed in the string B$.

1. Verify that 809 inverts to 608.

2. Only one of the following numbers does not invert. Which one is it?
   a. 666
   b. 880
   c. 009
   d. 818

3. Is 889,966 invertible? What about 6,666,666,666?

Modification Suggestions

☐ To find the number of invertible three-digit numbers, make these changes in the program in part A.

1. Add a counter to keep track of the number of invertible three-digit numbers. Choose a location C for the counter. Set C equal to zero at the beginning of the program. Add 1 to the counter after the PRINT statement that shows that A$ is invertible.

2. Now replace the INPUT statement with a FOR–NEXT loop to test all three-digit numbers. Because this program operates on strings rather than numbers, it is necessary to use one of your machine's special functions to convert the FOR–NEXT loop value to a string. The special function may differ from machine to machine. If necessary, consult your owner's manual.

3. Delete the PRINTs and replace them with one that shows the total, C, of three-digit invertible numbers. Place the PRINT statement just before the END statement.

Extensions

1. If Sam's number had been 808 instead of 809, he would have obtained the same number when he turned the card upside down. Numbers such as 808 and 906 are called *self-invertible numbers*. How many numbers between 100 and 999 are self-invertible, and what are they?

2. The 100th invertible number is a four-digit number. What is it?

3. If you consider the digit 1 to be invertible, additional numbers become invertible and the 100th invertible number is a three-digit number. What is it?

Notes

BASIC
PROGRAM SOLUTIONS
TO THE PROBLEMS

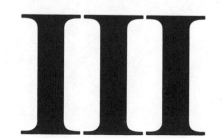

```
   3 REM   WRAPAROUND NUMBERS
  10 DIM A[4]
  20 FOR N=3000 TO 3999
  30    R=N
  40    FOR I=4 TO 1 STEP -1
  50      S=INT(R/10)
  60      A[I]=R-10*S
  70      R=S
  80    NEXT I
  90    K=1
 100    FOR I=1 TO 4
 110      IF A[K]=0 THEN 190
 120      S=K+A[K]
 130      A[K]=0
 140      K=S-4*INT((S-1)/4)
 150    NEXT I
 160    IF K<>1 THEN 190
 170    PRINT N
 190    GOTO 205
 205 NEXT N
 210 END




   3 REM   SUMS OF SQUARES
  20 PRINT "THE NUMBER   ";"FIRST SQUARE   ";"SECOND SQUARE"
  30 PRINT
  32 FOR N=1 TO 125
  34    C=0
  40    FOR A=1 TO INT(SQR(N))+1
  50      FOR B=1 TO A
  60        J=A*A+B*B
  70        IF J<>N THEN 90
  72        C=C+1
  74        IF C<>2 THEN 86
  80        PRINT N,A,B
  82        PRINT N,A1,B1
  86        A1=A
  88        B1=B
  90      NEXT B
 100    NEXT A
 105 NEXT N
 110 END
```

```
  3 REM   DOUBLE DEAL
 11 FOR N=6173 TO 9999
 20   S=0
 30   P=1
 40   R=N
 50   GOSUB 400
 60   M=2*N
 70   R=M
 80   GOSUB 400
 90   IF S<>285 THEN 120
100   IF P<>362880 THEN 120
110   PRINT N;" ITS DOUBLE ";M;" USE ALL 9 DIGITS"
115   GOTO 125
120 NEXT N
125 END
400 K=R/10
410 D=INT(10*(K-INT(K))+.5)
420 R=INT(K)
430 S=S+D*D
440 P=P*D
450 IF R<>0 THEN 400
460 RETURN


  3 REM   RECIPROCAL TRIPLES
  5 T=0
 10 INPUT N
 20 PRINT TAB(5);"A";TAB(12);"B";TAB(19);"C";TAB(30);"A+B+C"
 30 PRINT
 40 FOR A=1 TO N
 50   FOR B=1 TO A
 60     Z=((A*A*B*B)/(A*A+B*B))
 70     C=INT(SQR(Z))
 80     IF C*C<>Z THEN 100
 82     IF A+B+C>100 THEN 100
 90     PRINT TAB(5);A;TAB(12);B;TAB(19);C;TAB(30);A+B+C
 92     T=T+1
 94     IF T=2 THEN 120
100   NEXT B
110 NEXT A
120 END
```

```
  3 REM   CHAINS OF CONDENSED NUMBERS
 10 FOR N=10 TO 99
 12   X=0
 20   R=N
 30   C=0
 40   K=R/10
 50   D=INT(10*(K-INT(K))+.5)
 60   R=INT(K)
 70   C=C+D*D
 80   IF R<>0 THEN 40
 81   X=X+1
 82   IF C=37 THEN 94
 84   IF C=1 THEN 94
 86   R=C
 90   GOTO 30
 94   IF X<14 THEN 98
 96   PRINT N;" HAS CHAIN LENGTH ";X;" AND ENDS AT ";C
 98 NEXT N
100 END
```

```
  3 REM   WHAT'S THE ODOMETER READ?
 10 FOR X=100 TO 999
 20   Y=X*X-INT(X*X/1000)*1000
 25   IF X<>Y THEN 35
 30   PRINT X,X*Y,Y
 35 NEXT X
 40 END
```

```
  3 REM   ZIP CODES
 10 FOR A=1 TO 9
 20   FOR B=0 TO 9
 30     FOR C=0 TO 9
 40       P=(10*A+B)*1000+(C*100)+(10*B+A)
 43       S=A+B+C+B+A
 45       IF P/S<>1936 THEN 60
 50       PRINT P,S,P/S
 60     NEXT C
 70   NEXT B
 80 NEXT A
 90 END
```

139

```
  3 REM  TEMPERATURE TEASER
 10 FOR F=-100 TO 100
 20    C=5/9*(F-32)
 30    IF (C-INT(C))*10>=5 THEN 60
 40    C1=INT(C)
 50    GOTO 70
 60    C1=INT(C)+1
 70    IF F<>C1 THEN 75
 72    PRINT "C=";C1;" AND F=";F
 75 NEXT F
 80 END


  3 REM  MULTIPLY PERFECT NUMBERS
 10 FOR N=1 TO 1000
 15    S=0
 20    Q=SQR(N)
 30    FOR D1=1 TO Q
 40       D2=N/D1
 50       IF D2<>INT(D2) THEN 90
 60       IF D2=D1 THEN 80
 70       S=S+D2
 80       S=S+D1
 90    NEXT D1
 93    IF S/N<>INT(S/N) THEN 100
 95    PRINT "N=";N;" S=";S;" S/N=";S/N
100 NEXT N
110 END


  3 REM  LOCKER NUMBERS
 20 PRINT
 30 PRINT "X","Y","X*Y"
 40 PRINT
 45 FOR Y=2 TO 1000
 50    X=100*Y/(Y-1)
 52    IF X<>INT(X) THEN 65
 54    Z=INT(SQR(X*Y))
 56    IF X*Y<>Z*Z THEN 65
 57    IF X*Y<=1000 THEN 65
 59    IF X*Y>=10000 THEN 65
 60    PRINT X,Y,X*Y
 65 NEXT Y
 70 END
```

```
 3 REM  AGE ARRANGEMENTS
10 FOR X=1 TO 9
20   FOR Y=0 TO 9
30     FOR Z=0 TO 9
40       N=100*X+10*Y+Z
44       W=X+Y+Z
46       IF N/W<>29 THEN 60
50       PRINT N
60     NEXT Z
70   NEXT Y
80 NEXT X
90 END
```

```
 3 REM  THE MULTIPLIER EFFECT
10 FOR N=1000 TO 9999
20   R=0
30   P=N
40   K=P/10
50   P=INT(K)
60   D=INT(10*(K-P)+.5)
70   R=10*R+D
80   IF P<>0 THEN 40
82   IF R/N<>INT(R/N) THEN 95
84   IF R=N THEN 95
86   IF N=2178 THEN 95
92   PRINT N,R/N,R
94   GOTO 100
95 NEXT N
100 END
```

```
   3 REM   REVERSE AND ADD
  10 FOR N=10 TO 88
  15    C=0
  20    S=N
  30    Y=INT(LOG(S)/LOG(10))+1
  40    X=0
  50    R=S
  60    FOR A=1 TO Y
  70      K=R/10
  80      R=INT(K)
  90      D=INT(10*(K-R)+.5)
 100      X=10*X+D
 110    NEXT A
 115    IF S=X THEN 120
 116    S=S+X
 117    C=C+1
 118    GOTO 30
 120    IF C<>6 THEN 130
 125    PRINT N,C,X
 130 NEXT N
 140 END
```

```
   3 REM   DIFFERENT DIGITS
   5 T=0
  10 FOR A=1 TO 9
  20   FOR B=0 TO 9
  30     FOR C=0 TO 9
  40       IF (A-B)*(B-C)*(A-C)=0 THEN 90
  50       N=100*A+10*B+C
  60       S=(A+B+C)*(A+B+C)
  70       IF N/S-INT(N/S)<>0 THEN 90
  75       T=T+1
  80       PRINT N,S,N/S
  90     NEXT C
 100   NEXT B
 110 NEXT A
 114 PRINT
 115 PRINT "THE TOTAL IS ";T
 120 END
```

```
  3 REM   POSITIVE DIFFERENCES
 10 FOR I=0 TO 4
 15   FOR J=0 TO 4
 20     FOR K=0 TO 4
 23       FOR L=0 TO 4
 25         T=0
 26         A=I
 27         B=J
 28         C=K
 29         D=L
 40         E=A
 50         A=ABS(A-B)
 60         B=ABS(B-C)
 70         C=ABS(C-D)
 80         D=ABS(D-E)
 85         T=T+1
 93         IF A+B+C+D<>0 THEN 40
 94         IF T<7 THEN 96
 95         PRINT I;J;K;L,
 96       NEXT L
 97     NEXT K
 98   NEXT J
 99 NEXT I
100 END
400 PRINT A
410 PRINT TAB(9);B
420 PRINT TAB(17);C
430 PRINT TAB(25);D
435 PRINT T
440 RETURN


  3 REM   HOW MANY JELLY BEANS?
 10 FOR X=1 TO 10000
 30   IF X-7*INT(X/7)<>1 THEN 70
 40   IF X-9*INT(X/9)<>2 THEN 70
 50   IF X-11*INT(X/11)<>5 THEN 70
 55   Z=INT(SQR(X-56))
 56   IF (X-56)<>Z*Z THEN 70
 60   PRINT X
 70 NEXT X
 80 END
```

```
 3 REM   ARRANGING SOLDIERS
10 FOR N=1 TO 200
14   M=INT(SQR(N))
15   IF M*M=N THEN 65
20   FOR Y=1 TO 3000
30     X=INT(SQR(N*Y*Y+1))
40     IF X*X=N*Y*Y+1 THEN 60
50   NEXT Y
60   PRINT "N=";N,N*Y*Y;" SOLDIERS"
62   IF N*Y*Y>100000 THEN 70
65 NEXT N
70 END
```

```
  3 REM   THE DECADE OF THE 1980'S
  5 T=0
 10 A=1
 15 B=9
 17 C=8
 20 FOR D=0 TO 9
 30   FOR E=0 TO 9
 40     FOR F=0 TO 9
 50       G=10*A+E
 60       H=10*B+F
 70       P=G*F
 80       Q=G*B
 90       IF Q<100 THEN 200
100       IF INT(P/10)<>C THEN 200
110       IF Q-10*INT(Q/10)<>D THEN 200
120       PRINT
130       PRINT TAB(6);G
140       PRINT TAB(6);H
150       PRINT TAB(5);"---"
160       PRINT TAB(6);P
170       PRINT TAB(4);Q
180       PRINT TAB(4);"---"
190       PRINT TAB(4);G*H
195       T=T+1
200     NEXT F
210   NEXT E
215 NEXT D
219 PRINT T
220 END
```

144

```
  3 REM   SQUARE DIFFERENCES
 10 FOR N=1 TO 999
 15    C=0
 20    FOR Y=0 TO N
 30       X=INT(SQR(N+Y*Y)+.5)
 40       IF X*X<>N+Y*Y THEN 60
 55       C=C+1
 60    NEXT Y
 65    IF C=3 THEN 75
 70 NEXT N
 75 PRINT N;" TILES TODAY"
 80 END


  3 REM   INVERTIBLE NUMBERS
  5 C=0
 10 FOR Z=0 TO 999
 15    A$=STR$(Z)
 20    B$=""
 30    L=LEN(A$)
 40    FOR J=L TO 1 STEP -1
 50       D$=MID(A$,J,1)
 60       IF D$<>"6" AND D$<>"9" THEN 120
 70       IF D$="6" THEN 100
 80       D$="6"
 90       GOTO 130
100       D$="9"
110       GOTO 130
120       IF D$<>"8" AND D$<>"0" THEN 170
130       B$=B$+D$
140    NEXT J
155    C=C+1
170 NEXT Z
175 PRINT C;" NUMBERS ARE INVERTIBLE"
180 END
```

NUMERICAL ANSWERS
TO THE PROBLEMS

1. WRAPAROUND NUMBERS

There are 20 wraparound numbers beginning with the digit 3. They are: 3122, 3126, 3162, 3166, 3333, 3337, 3373, 3377, 3522, 3526, 3562, 3566, 3733, 3737, 3773, 3777, 3922, 3926, 3962, and 3966.

2. SUMS OF SQUARES

The following table gives the whole numbers of less than 125 that are the sums of two squares in two different ways.

Number	First Square	Second Square
50	7	1
50	5	5
65	8	1
65	7	4
85	9	2
85	7	6

3. DOUBLE DEAL

The smallest four-digit number giving a "double" deal is 6729. Its double, 13,458, uses all nine digits.

4. RECIPROCAL TRIPLES

The two reciprocal triples with sums of less than 100 are 20, 15, 12 and 40, 30, 24, which have the sums 47 and 94, respectively.

5. CHAINS OF CONDENSED NUMBERS

There are four two-digit numbers with chains of 14 or more. They are 36 with chain length 14, 60 with chain length 15, 63 with chain length 14, and 99 with chain length 14. Each chain ends at 37.

6. WHAT'S THE ODOMETER READ?

Laurie traveled either 376 or 625 miles, since the square of 376 is 141,376 and the square of 625 is 390,625.

7. ZIP CODES

There are three five-digit palindromes that equal 1936 when divided by the sums of their digits. They are: 23,232, 46,464, and 69,696.

8. TEMPERATURE TEASER

The three Fahrenheit temperatures for which the Celsius temperature is the same are −41, −40, and −39 degrees.

9. MULTIPLY PERFECT NUMBERS

The table gives the six multiply perfect numbers N less than 1000 with the corresponding values of S and S/N.

N	S	S/N
1	1	1
6	12	2
28	56	2
120	360	3
496	992	2
672	2016	3

10. LOCKER NUMBERS

Beth and Bob's locker numbers were 104 and 26 and the number of students at the school was 2704.

11. AGE ARRANGEMENTS

Sarah's children were age, 2, 6, and 1, and the three-digit number formed was 261.

12. THE MULTIPLIER EFFECT

The multiplier was 9 and the four-digit multiplicand was 1089, giving the product 9801.

13. REVERSE AND ADD

The integer 79 requires six additions before a palindrome, 44,044, is reached.

14. DIFFERENT DIGITS

There are 10 three-digit numbers with no repeating digits which have no remainder when divided by the square of the sums of their digits. They are: 162, 243, 324, 392, 405, 512, 605, 648, 810, and 972.

15. POSITIVE DIFFERENCES

There are 16 sets of four digits, no digit of which is bigger than 4, which require repeating the process of taking positive differences seven times before reaching 0, 0, 0, 0. They are: 0124, 0234, 0421, 0432, 1042, 1240, 2043, 2104, 2340, 2401, 3204, 3402, 4012, 4023, 4210, and 4320.

16. HOW MANY JELLY BEANS?

There were either 3305 or 8156 jelly beans.

17. ARRANGING SOLDIERS IN SQUARES

The smallest number you could choose and have the number of soldiers be more than 100,000 is $N = 13$, which gives 421,200 soldiers.

18. THE DECADE OF THE 1980s

There are four solutions to the problem. They are:

17	16	14	12
95	95	96	97
85	80	84	84
153	144	126	108
1615	1520	1344	1164

19. SQUARE DIFFERENCES

The fewest number of mauve, maize, and magenta tiles that Mandy could have at the end of the day is 45.

20. INVERTIBLE NUMBERS

There are 64 three-digit numbers that are invertible.

BASIC PROGRAM
SOLUTIONS
TO THE EXTENSIONS

```
  3 REM   WRAPAROUND NUMBERS E1
 10 DIM A(4)
 20 FOR N=1900 TO 1999
 30    R=N
 40    FOR I=4 TO 1 STEP -1
 50      S=INT(R/10)
 60      A(I)=R-10*S
 70      R=S
 80    NEXT I
 90    K=1
100    FOR I=1 TO 4
110      IF A(K)=0 THEN 190
120      S=K+A(K)
130      A(K)=0
140      K=S-4*INT((S-1)/4)
150    NEXT I
160    IF K<>1 THEN 190
170    PRINT N
190    GOTO 205
205 NEXT N
210 END


  3 REM   WRAPAROUND NUMBERS E2
  8 T=0
 10 DIM A(4)
 20 FOR N=1000 TO 9999
 30    R=N
 40    FOR I=4 TO 1 STEP -1
 50      S=INT(R/10)
 60      A(I)=R-10*S
 70      R=S
 80    NEXT I
 90    K=1
100    FOR I=1 TO 4
110      IF A(K)=0 THEN 190
120      S=K+A(K)
130      A(K)=0
140      K=S-4*INT((S-1)/4)
150    NEXT I
160    IF K<>1 THEN 190
170    PRINT N
180    T=T+1
190    GOTO 205
205 NEXT N
208 PRINT "THERE ARE ";T;" WRAPAROUND NUMBERS"
210 END
```

```
  3 REM   WRAPAROUND NUMBERS E3
  8 T=0
 10 DIM A(3)
 20 FOR N=100 TO 999
 30   R=N
 40   FOR I=3 TO 1 STEP -1
 50     S=INT(R/10)
 60     A(I)=R-10*S
 70     R=S
 80   NEXT I
 90   K=1
100   FOR I=1 TO 3
110     IF A(K)=0 THEN 190
120     S=K+A(K)
130     A(K)=0
140     K=S-3*INT((S-1)/3)
150   NEXT I
160   IF K<>1 THEN 190
170   PRINT N
180   T=T+1
190   GOTO 205
205 NEXT N
208 PRINT "THERE ARE ";T;" WRAPAROUND NUMBERS WITH 3 DIGITS"
210 END
```

```
  3 REM   SUMS OF SQUARES E1
 30 PRINT
 31 K=1
 32 FOR N=1 TO 9999
 34   C=0
 40   FOR A=1 TO INT(SQR(N))+1
 50     FOR B=1 TO A
 60       J=A*A+B*B
 70       IF J<>N THEN 90
 72       C=C+1
 74       IF C<>K THEN 86
 80       PRINT N;"IS THE SMALLEST NUMBER THAT IS"
 82       PRINT "THE SUM OF TWO SQUARES IN ";K;" WAYS"
 83       PRINT
 84       K=K+1
 85       GOTO 105
 86       A1=A
 88       B1=B
 90     NEXT B
100   NEXT A
105 NEXT N
110 END
```

```
  3 REM   SUMS OF SQUARES E2
 31 K=1
 32 FOR N=1 TO 9999
 34   C=0
 40   FOR A=1 TO INT(SQR(N))+1
 50     FOR B=1 TO A-1
 60       J=A*A+B*B
 70       IF J<>N THEN 90
 72       C=C+1
 74       IF C<>2 THEN 86
 80       PRINT N;" = ";A;"*";A;" + ";B;"*";B
 82       PRINT N;" = ";A1;"*";A1;" + ";B1;"*";B1
 85       GOTO 110
 86       A1=A
 88       B1=B
 90     NEXT B
100   NEXT A
105 NEXT N
110 END


  3 REM   SUMS OF SQUARES E3
 31 K=1
 32 FOR N=1 TO 9999
 34   C=0
 40   FOR A=1 TO INT(SQR(N))+1
 50     FOR B=1 TO A-1
 60       J=A*A+B*B
 70       IF J<>N THEN 90
 72       C=C+1
 74       IF C<>3 THEN 86
 80       PRINT N;" = ";A;"*";A;" + ";B;"*";B
 82       PRINT N;" = ";A1;"*";A1;" + ";B1;"*";B1
 84       PRINT N;" = ";A2;"*";A2;" + ";B2;"*";B2
 85       GOTO 110
 86       A2=A1
 87       B2=B1
 88       A1=A
 89       B1=B
 90     NEXT B
100   NEXT A
105 NEXT N
110 END
```

```
  3 REM   DOUBLE DEAL E1
  9 PRINT "WHAT MULTIPLE";
 10 INPUT Z
 11 FOR N=INT(12345/Z) TO INT(99999/Z)
 20   S=0
 30   P=1
 40   R=N
 50   GOSUB 400
 60   M=Z*N
 70   R=M
 80   GOSUB 400
 90   IF S<>285 THEN 120
100   IF P<>362880 THEN 120
110   PRINT N;" AND ITS MULTIPLE ";M;" USE ALL 9 DIGITS"
120 NEXT N
125 END
400 K=R/10
410 D=INT(10*(K-INT(K))+.5)
420 R=INT(K)
430 S=S+D*D
440 P=P*D
450 IF R<>0 THEN 400
460 RETURN
```

```
  3 REM   DOUBLE DEAL E2
 11 FOR N=686 TO 5555
 20   S=0
 30   P=1
 40   R=N
 50   GOSUB 400
 60   M=18*N
 70   R=M
 80   GOSUB 400
 90   IF S<>285 THEN 120
100   IF P<>362880 THEN 120
110   PRINT N;" ITS DOUBLE ";M;" USE ALL 9 DIGITS"
120 NEXT N
125 END
400 K=R/10
410 D=INT(10*(K-INT(K))+.5)
420 R=INT(K)
430 S=S+D*D
440 P=P*D
450 IF R<>0 THEN 400
460 RETURN
```

```
  3 REM   DOUBLE DEAL E3
  9 FOR Z=2 TO 99
 11   FOR N=INT(12345/Z) TO INT(99999/Z)
 20     S=0
 30     P=1
 40     R=N
 50     GOSUB 400
 60     M=Z*N
 70     R=M
 80     GOSUB 400
 90     IF S<>285 THEN 120
100     IF P<>362880 THEN 120
110     PRINT Z;"   ";
111     N=99999
120   NEXT N
123 NEXT Z
125 END
400 K=R/10
410 D=INT(10*(K-INT(K))+.5)
420 R=INT(K)
430 S=S+D*D
440 P=P*D
450 IF R<>0 THEN 400
460 RETURN


  3 REM   RECIPROCAL TRIPLES E1
 10 INPUT N
 20 PRINT TAB(5);"A";TAB(12);"B";TAB(19);"C";TAB(30);"A+B+C"
 30 PRINT
 40 FOR A=2 TO N
 50   FOR B=1 TO A-1
 55     P=SQR(A)
 56     Q=SQR(B)
 60     Z=P*Q/(P+Q)
 70     C=Z*Z
 80     IF C<>INT(C) THEN 100
 90     PRINT TAB(5);A;TAB(12);B;TAB(19);C;TAB(30);A+B+C
100   NEXT B
110 NEXT A
120 END
```

```
 3 REM   CHAINS OF CONDENSED NUMBERS E1
 6 M=1
 7 PRINT "HOW MANY DIGITS";
 8 INPUT Z
 9 W=INT(10^(Z-1)+.5)
10 FOR N=W TO 10*W-1
12    X=0
20    R=N
30    C=0
40    K=R/10
50    D=INT(10*(K-INT(K))+.5)
60    R=INT(K)
70    C=C+D*D
80    IF R<>0 THEN 40
81    X=X+1
82    IF C=37 THEN 94
84    IF C=1 THEN 94
86    R=C
90    GOTO 30
94    IF X<=M THEN 98
95    M=X
98 NEXT N
99 PRINT "THE LONGEST CHAIN LENGTH FOR AN ";Z;" DIGIT NUMBER IS ";M
100 END
```

```
 3 REM   CHAINS OF CONDENSED NUMBERS E2
10 FOR N=10 TO 99
12    X=0
20    R=N
30    C=0
40    K=R/10
50    D=INT(10*(K-INT(K))+.5)
60    R=INT(K)
70    C=C+D*D
80    IF R<>0 THEN 40
81    X=X+1
82    IF C=37 THEN 98
84    IF C=1 THEN 96
86    R=C
90    GOTO 30
94    IF X<>4 THEN 98
96    PRINT N;" HAS CHAIN LENGTH ";X;" AND ENDS AT ";C
98 NEXT N
100 END
```

```
  3 REM   RECIPROCAL TRIPLES E2
 10 INPUT N
 20 PRINT TAB(5);"A";TAB(12);"B";TAB(19);"C";TAB(30);"A+B+C"
 30 PRINT
 40 FOR A=2 TO N
 50   FOR B=1 TO A
 55     P=A
 56     Q=B
 60     Z=A*B/(A+B)
 70     C=Z
 80     IF C<>INT(C) THEN 100
 90       PRINT TAB(5);A;TAB(12);B;TAB(19);C;TAB(30);A+B+C
100   NEXT B
110 NEXT A
120 END


  3 REM   RECIPROCAL TRIPLES E3
 10 INPUT N
 20 PRINT TAB(4);"A";TAB(9);"B";TAB(14);"C";TAB(19);"D";TAB(30);
   "A+B+C+D"
 30 PRINT
 40 FOR A=1 TO N
 50   FOR B=1 TO A
 52     FOR C=1 TO B
 55       P=A*A
 56       Q=B*B
 58       R=C*C
 60       Z=P*Q*R/(((P+Q)*R)+P*Q)
 70       D=INT(SQR(Z)+.5)
 80       IF D*D<>Z THEN 98
 82       IF A+B+C>100 THEN 100
 90         PRINT TAB(4);A;TAB(9);B;TAB(14);C;TAB(19);D;TAB(30);A+B+C+D
 98     NEXT C
100   NEXT B
110 NEXT A
120 END
```

```
  3 REM   CHAINS OF CONDENSED NUMBERS E3
  7 T=0
 10 FOR N=100 TO 999
 12    X=0
 20    R=N
 30    C=0
 40    K=R/10
 50    D=INT(10*(K-INT(K))+.5)
 60    R=INT(K)
 70    C=C+D*D
 80    IF R<>0 THEN 40
 81    X=X+1
 82    IF C=37 THEN 94
 84    IF C=1 THEN 94
 86    R=C
 90    GOTO 30
 94    IF X<15 THEN 98
 95    T=T+1
 98 NEXT N
 99 PRINT "THERE ARE ";T;
    " THREE DIGIT NUMBERS WITH CHAINS OF LENGTH AT LEAST 15"
100 END
```

```
 3 REM   WHAT'S THE ODOMETER READ? E1
10 FOR X=100 TO 999
20    Y=X*X-INT(X*X/1000)*1000
25    IF 2*X<>Y THEN 35
30    PRINT X,X*X,Y
35 NEXT X
40 END
```

```
 3 REM   WHAT'S THE ODOMETER READ? E2
 7 PRINT
 8 FOR K=3 TO 5
 9    PRINT "FOR A MULTIPLE OF ";K;"   :"
10    FOR X=100 TO 999
20       Y=X*X-INT(X*X/1000)*1000
25       IF K*X<>Y THEN 35
30       PRINT X,X*X,Y
35    NEXT X
36    PRINT
37 NEXT K
40 END
```

```
 3 REM   WHAT'S THE ODOMETER READ? E3
10 FOR X=100 TO 999
20    I=.1
25    FOR J=0 TO 3
30       I=I*10
40       Z=INT(X*X/I)
50       Y=Z-INT(Z/1000)*1000
60       IF X=Y THEN PRINT X,X*X,I
70    NEXT J
80 NEXT X
```

```
 3 REM   ZIP CODES E1
 7 T=0
10 FOR A=1 TO 9
20    FOR B=0 TO 9
30      FOR C=0 TO 9
40        P=(10*A+B)*1000+(C*100)+(10*B+A)
43        S=A+B+C+B+A
45        IF P/S<>INT(P/S) THEN 60
50        PRINT P,S,P/S
55        T=T+1
60      NEXT C
70    NEXT B
80 NEXT A
82 PRINT
84 PRINT "THERE ARE ";T;" OF THESE NUMBERS"
90 END
```

```
 3 REM   ZIP CODES E2
 7 T=0
10 FOR A=1 TO 9
20    FOR B=A TO A
30      FOR C=0 TO 9
40        P=(10*A+B)*1000+(C*100)+(10*B+A)
43        S=A+B+C+B+A
45        IF P/S<>INT(P/S) THEN 60
50        PRINT P,S,P/S
55        T=T+1
60      NEXT C
70    NEXT B
80 NEXT A
82 PRINT
84 PRINT "THERE ARE ";T;" OF THESE NUMBERS"
90 END
```

```
  3 REM   ZIP CODES E3
  7 T=0
 10 FOR A=1 TO 9
 20    FOR B=0 TO 9
 40       P=(10*A+B)*100+(10*B+A)
 43       S=A+B+B+A
 45       IF P/S<>INT(P/S) THEN 70
 50       PRINT P,S,P/S
 55       T=T+1
 70    NEXT B
 80 NEXT A
 82 PRINT
 84 PRINT "THERE ARE ";T;" OF THESE NUMBERS"
 90 END
```

```
  3 REM   TEMPERATURE TEASER E1
 10 FOR F=150 TO 200
 20    C=5/9*(F-32)
 30    IF (C-INT(C))*10>=5 THEN 60
 40    C1=INT(C)
 50    GOTO 65
 60    C1=INT(C)+1
 65    F1=F-INT(F/100)*100
 70    IF F1<>C1 THEN 75
 72    PRINT "C=";C1;" AND F=";F
 75 NEXT F
 80 END
```

```
  3 REM   TEMPERATURE TEASER E2
 10 FOR F=10 TO 99
 20    C=5/9*(F-32)
 30    IF (C-INT(C))*10>=5 THEN 60
 40    C1=INT(C)
 50    GOTO 65
 60    C1=INT(C)+1
 65    P=INT(F/10)
 66    Q=F-P*10
 67    F1=10*Q+P
 70    IF F1<>C1 THEN 75
 72    PRINT "C=";C1;" AND F=";F
 75 NEXT F
 80 END
```

```
  3 REM   TEMPERATURE TEASER E3
 10 FOR F=100 TO 999
 20    C=5/9*(F-32)
 30    IF (C-INT(C))*10>=5 THEN 60
 40    C1=INT(C)
 50    GOTO 63
 60    C1=INT(C)+1
 63    F0=F-INT(F/100)*100
 65    P=INT(F0/10)
 66    Q=F0-P*10
 67    F1=10*Q+P
 70    IF F1<>C1 THEN 75
 72    PRINT "C=";C1;" AND F=";F
 75 NEXT F
 80 END
```

```
  3 REM   MULTIPLY PERFECT NUMBERS E1
 10 FOR N=1 TO 999 STEP 2
 15    S=0
 20    Q=SQR(N)
 30    FOR D1=1 TO Q
 40       D2=N/D1
 50       IF D2<>INT(D2) THEN 90
 60       IF D2=D1 THEN 80
 70       S=S+D2
 80       S=S+D1
 90    NEXT D1
 93    IF S/N<=2 THEN 100
 95    PRINT "N=";N;" S=";S;" S/N=";S/N
 97    GOTO 110
100 NEXT N
110 END
```

```
  3 REM   MULTIPLY PERFECT NUMBERS E2
 10 FOR N=1 TO 100
 15    T=0
 20    Q=SQR(N)
 30    FOR D1=1 TO Q
 40       D2=N/D1
 50       IF D2<>INT(D2) THEN 90
 60       IF D2=D1 THEN 80
 70       T=T+1
 80       T=T+1
 90    NEXT D1
 93    IF N/T<>INT(N/T) THEN 100
 95    PRINT "N=";N;" T=";T;" N/T=";N/T
100 NEXT N
110 END
```

```
  3 REM   MULTIPLY PERFECT NUMBERS E3
  8 K=0
 10 FOR N=1 TO 100
 15   T=0
 20   Q=SQR(N)
 30   FOR D1=1 TO Q
 40     D2=N/D1
 50     IF D2<>INT(D2) THEN 90
 60     IF D2=D1 THEN 80
 70     T=T+1
 80     T=T+1
 90   NEXT D1
 93   IF T/2=INT(T/2) THEN 100
 95   PRINT N;" HAS ";T;" DIVISORS "
 96   K=K+1
100 NEXT N
105 PRINT
106 PRINT K;" NUMBERS HAVE AN ODD NUMBER OF DIVISORS"
110 END
```

```
  3 REM   LOCKER NUMBERS E1
 20 PRINT
 30 PRINT "X","Y","X*Y"
 40 PRINT
 45 FOR Y=2 TO 222
 50   X=110*Y/(Y-1)
 53   IF X<>INT(X) THEN 65
 55   IF X+Y<>222 THEN 65
 60   PRINT X,Y,X*Y
 65 NEXT Y
 70 END
```

```
  3 REM   LOCKER NUMBERS E2
 20 PRINT
 30 PRINT "X","Y","Z"
 40 PRINT
 45 FOR Y=2 TO 100
 47   FOR Z=1 TO 100
 50     X=(10*Y+100*Z)/(Y*Z-1)
 52     IF X<>INT(X) THEN 65
 54     W=INT(SQR(X*Y*Z-5)+.5)
 56     IF W*W<>X*Y*Z-5 THEN 65
 60     PRINT X,Y,Z
 65   NEXT Z
 67 NEXT Y
 70 END
```

```
 3 REM   LOCKER NUMBERS E3
20 PRINT
30 PRINT "X","Y","Z"
40 PRINT
45 FOR Y=2 TO 1000
47    Z=Y+1
50    X=(10*Y+100*Z)/(Y*Z-1)
52    IF X<>INT(X) THEN 65
55    IF X<>Y-1 THEN 65
60    PRINT X,Y,Z
65 NEXT Y
70 END
```

```
 3 REM   AGE ARRANGEMENTS E1
 4 INPUT "K = ";K
 5 FOR P=1 TO 9
10    FOR X=1 TO 9
20       FOR Y=0 TO 9
30          FOR Z=0 TO 9
40             N=1000*P+100*X*10*Y+Z
44             W=P+X+Y+Z
46             IF N/W<>K THEN 60
50             PRINT N
60          NEXT Z
70       NEXT Y
80    NEXT X
85 NEXT P
90 END
```

```
 3 REM   AGE ARRANGEMENTS E2
 4 INPUT "K = ";K
 5 FOR P=0 TO 0
10    FOR X=10 TO 19
20       FOR Y=0 TO 0
30          FOR Z=10 TO 19
40             N=1000*P+100*X+10*Y+Z
44             W=P+X+Y+Z
46             IF N/W<>K THEN 60
50             PRINT N
60          NEXT Z
70       NEXT Y
80    NEXT X
85 NEXT P
90 END
```

```
 3 REM   AGE ARRANGEMENTS E3
10 FOR X=10 TO 24
20    FOR Y=10 TO 24
30      FOR Z=1 TO 9
40        N=1000*X+10*Y+Z
44        W=X*Y*Z
46        IF N/W<>14 THEN 60
50        PRINT N
60      NEXT Z
70    NEXT Y
80 NEXT X
90 END
```

```
 3 REM   THE MULTIPLIER EFFECT E1
10 FOR N=10000 TO 50000
20    R=0
30    P=N
40    K=P/10
50    P=INT(K)
60    D=INT(10*(K-P)+.5)
70    R=10*R+D
80    IF P<>0 THEN 40
82    IF R/N<>INT(R/N) THEN 95
84    IF R=N THEN 95
92    PRINT N,R/N,R
95 NEXT N
100 END
```

```
 3 REM   THE MULTIPLIER EFFECT E2
10 FOR N=10000 TO 50000
20    L=INT(N/1000)
30    M=N-L*1000
40    P=INT(L/10)
50    Q=L-P*10
60    R=100*M+10*Q+P
82    IF R/N<>INT(R/N) THEN 95
84    IF R=N THEN 95
92    PRINT N,R/N,R
95 NEXT N
100 END
```

```
  3 REM   THE MULTIPLIER EFFECT E3
 10 FOR N=1000 TO 5000
 20   L=INT(N/100)
 30   M=N-L*100
 40   P=INT(L/10)
 50   Q=L-P*10
 60   R=100*M+10*Q+P
 82   IF R/N<>INT(R/N) THEN 95
 84   IF R=N THEN 95
 92   PRINT N,R/N,R
 95 NEXT N
100 END
```

```
  3 REM   REVERSE AND ADD E1
 10 FOR N=10 TO 99
 15   C=0
 20   S=N
 30   Y=INT(LOG(S)/LOG(10))+1
 40   X=0
 50   R=S
 60   FOR A=1 TO Y
 70     K=R/10
 80     R=INT(K)
 90     D=INT(10*(K-R)+.5)
100     X=10*X+D
110   NEXT A
115   IF S=X THEN 125
116   S=S+X
117   C=C+1
118   GOTO 30
125   PRINT N,C,X
130 NEXT N
140 END
```

```
  3 REM   REVERSE  AND  ADD  E2
  8 T=1
 10 FOR N=10 TO 99
 15    C=0
 20    S=N
 30    Y=INT(LOG(S)/LOG(10))+1
 40    X=0
 50    R=S
 60    FOR  A=1  TO  Y
 70      K=R/10
 80      R=INT(K)
 90      D=INT(10*(K-R)+.5)
100      X=10*X+D
110    NEXT  A
115    IF  S=X  THEN  125
116    S=S+X
117    C=C+1
118    GOTO 30
125    IF  C<T  THEN  130
126    PRINT  N,C,X
127    T=T+1
130 NEXT  N
140 END
```

```
  3 REM   REVERSE  AND  ADD  E3
 10 FOR N=100 TO 999
 15    C=0
 20    S=N
 30    Y=INT(LOG(S)/LOG(10))+1
 40    X=0
 50    R=S
 60    FOR  A=1  TO  Y
 70      K=R/10
 80      R=INT(K)
 90      D=INT(10*(K-R)+.5)
100      X=10*X+D
110    NEXT  A
115    IF  S=X  THEN  125
116    S=S+X
117    C=C+1
118    GOTO 30
125    IF  X/11=INT(X/11)  THEN  130
126    PRINT  N,C,X
127    T=T+1
130 NEXT  N
140 END
```

```
  3 REM   DIFFERENT DIGITS E1
  5 T=0
 10 FOR A=1 TO 9
 20   FOR B=0 TO 9
 30     FOR C=0 TO 9
 40       IF (A-B)*(B-C)*(A-C)<>0 THEN 90
 50       N=100*A+10*B+C
 60       S=(A+B+C)*(A+B+C)
 70       IF N/S-INT(N/S)<>0 THEN 90
 75       T=T+1
 80       PRINT N,S,N/S
 90     NEXT C
100   NEXT B
110 NEXT A
114 PRINT
115 PRINT "THE TOTAL IS ";T
120 END


  3 REM   DIFFERENT DIGITS E2
  5 T=0
 10 FOR A=1 TO 9
 20   FOR B=0 TO 9
 30     FOR C=0 TO 9
 40       IF (A-B)*(B-C)*(A-C)=0 THEN 90
 42       FOR D=0 TO 9
 44         IF (A-D)*(B-D)*(C-D)=0 THEN 88
 75         T=T+1
 88       NEXT D
 90     NEXT C
100   NEXT B
110 NEXT A
114 PRINT
115 PRINT "THE TOTAL IS ";T
120 END
```

```
  3 REM    DIFFERENT DIGITS E3
  5 T=0
 10 FOR A=1 TO 9
 20    FOR B=0 TO 9
 30      FOR C=0 TO 9
 40        IF (A-B)*(B-C)*(A-C)=0 THEN 90
 42        FOR D=0 TO 9
 44          IF (A-D)*(B-D)*(C-D)=0 THEN 88
 50          N=100*A+10*B+C
 55          N=10*N+D
 60          S=(A+B+C+D)*(A+B+C+D)
 70          IF N/S-INT(N/S)<>0 THEN 88
 75          T=T+1
 80          PRINT N,S,N/S
 88        NEXT D
 90      NEXT C
100    NEXT B
110 NEXT A
114 PRINT
115 PRINT "THE TOTAL IS ";T
120 END


  3 REM    POSITIVE DIFFERENCES E1
 10 FOR I=0 TO 9
 15    FOR J=0 TO 9
 20      FOR K=0 TO 9
 23        FOR L=0 TO 9
 25          T=0
 26          A=I
 27          B=J
 28          C=K
 29          D=L
 40          E=A
 50          A=ABS(A-B)
 60          B=ABS(B-C)
 70          C=ABS(C-D)
 80          D=ABS(D-E)
 85          T=T+1
 93          IF A+B+C+D<>0 THEN 40
 94          IF T<8 THEN 96
 95          PRINT I;J;K;L,"T=";T
 96        NEXT L
 97      NEXT K
 98    NEXT J
 99 NEXT I
100 GOTO 500
400 PRINT A
410 PRINT TAB(9);B
420 PRINT TAB(17);C
430 PRINT TAB(25);D
435 PRINT T
440 RETURN
500 END
```

```
  3 REM   POSITIVE DIFFERENCES E2
 10 INPUT I
 25 T=0
 26 A=I
 27 B=2*I
 28 C=3*I
 29 D=4*I
 40 E=A
 50 A=ABS(A-B)
 60 B=ABS(B-C)
 70 C=ABS(C-D)
 80 D=ABS(D-E)
 85 T=T+1
 93 IF A+B+C+D<>0 THEN 40
 95 PRINT I;I*2;I*3;I*4,"T=";T
100 GOTO 500
400 PRINT A
410 PRINT TAB(9);B
420 PRINT TAB(17);C
430 PRINT TAB(25);D
435 PRINT T
440 RETURN
500 END
```

```
  3 REM   POSITIVE DIFFERENCES E3
 10 INPUT I
 25 T=0
 26 A=I
 27 B=3+I
 28 C=6+I
 29 D=9+I
 40 E=A
 50 A=ABS(A-B)
 60 B=ABS(B-C)
 70 C=ABS(C-D)
 80 D=ABS(D-E)
 85 T=T+1
 93 IF A+B+C+D<>0 THEN 40
 95 PRINT I;I+3;I+6;I+9,"T=";T
100 GOTO 500
400 PRINT A
410 PRINT TAB(9);B
420 PRINT TAB(17);C
430 PRINT TAB(25);D
435 PRINT T
440 RETURN
500 END
```

```
  3 REM   HOW MANY JELLY BEANS? E1
 10 FOR X=10000 TO 1 STEP -1
 30    IF X-5*INT(X/5)<>4 THEN 70
 40    IF X-7*INT(X/7)<>5 THEN 70
 50    IF X-9*INT(X/9)<>6 THEN 70
 60    PRINT X
 65    GOTO 80
 70 NEXT X
 80 END
```

```
  3 REM   HOW MANY JELLY BEANS? E2
 10 FOR X=1900 TO 1939
 15    IF X-3*INT(X/3)<>1 THEN 70
 20    IF X-4*INT(X/4)<>2 THEN 70
 25    IF X-5*INT(X/5)<>3 THEN 70
 30    IF X-6*INT(X/6)<>4 THEN 70
 35    Y=X+60
 40    IF Y-3*INT(Y/3)<>1 THEN 70
 45    IF Y-4*INT(Y/4)<>2 THEN 70
 50    IF Y-5*INT(Y/5)<>3 THEN 70
 55    IF Y-6*INT(Y/6)<>4 THEN 70
 60    PRINT "AGES ARE ";X;" AND ";Y
 70 NEXT X
 80 END
```

```
  3 REM   HOW MANY JELLY BEANS? E3
  6 FOR I=1 TO 4
  7    S=0
  8    READ A,B,C,D
  9    READ E,F,G,H
 10    FOR X=1 TO 10000
 20       IF X-A*INT(X/A)<>E THEN 70
 30       IF X-B*INT(X/B)<>F THEN 70
 40       IF X-C*INT(X/C)<>G THEN 70
 50       IF X-D*INT(X/D)<>H THEN 70
 62       S=1
 70    NEXT X
 72    DATA 3,5,7,9
 73    DATA 1,2,3,4
 74    DATA 6,7,8,9
 75    DATA 1,2,3,4
 76    DATA 3,5,8,10
 77    DATA 1,2,3,4
 78    DATA 3,5,7,9
 79    DATA 2,4,6,8
 80    IF S=1 THEN 90
 85    PRINT A;"   ";B;"   ";C;"   ";D
 87    PRINT
 89    PRINT E;"   ";F;"   ";G;"   ";H
 90 NEXT I
100 END
```

174

```
 3 REM   ARRANGING SOLDIERS E1
10 FOR N=1 TO 200
14    M=INT(SQR(N))
15    IF M*M=N THEN 65
20    FOR Y=1 TO 3000
30       X=INT(SQR(N*Y*Y+1))
40       IF X*X=N*Y*Y+1 THEN 60
50    NEXT Y
60    PRINT "N=";N,N*Y*Y;" SOLDIERS"
62    IF N*Y*Y>1000000 THEN 70
65 NEXT N
70 END
```

```
 3 REM   ARRANGING SOLDIERS E2
 5 K=1
10 FOR N=1 TO 200
14    M=INT(SQR(N))
15    IF M*M=N THEN 65
20    FOR Y=1 TO 200
25       IF N*Y*Y+K<0 THEN 50
30       X=INT(SQR(N*Y*Y+K))
40       IF X*X=N*Y*Y+K THEN 60
50    NEXT Y
51    PRINT "N=";N,"******* SOLDIERS"
52    GOTO 65
60    IF Y<>1 THEN 65
62    PRINT "N=";N,N*Y*Y;" SOLDIERS"
65 NEXT N
70 END
```

```
 3 REM   ARRANGING SOLDIERS E3
 5 K=1
10 FOR N=1 TO 200
14    M=INT(SQR(N))
15    IF M*M=N THEN 65
20    FOR Y=1 TO 200
25       IF N*Y*Y+K<0 THEN 50
30       X=INT(SQR(N*Y*Y+K))
40       IF X*X=N*Y*Y+K THEN 60
50    NEXT Y
51    PRINT "N=";N,"******* SOLDIERS"
52    GOTO 65
60    IF Y<>2 THEN 65
62    PRINT "N=";N,N*Y*Y;" SOLDIERS"
65 NEXT N
70 END
```

```
  3 REM    THE DECADE OF THE 1980'S E1
  5 T=0
 10 A=1
 15 B=9
 20 FOR C=0 TO 9
 25    FOR D=0 TO 9
 30       FOR E=0 TO 9
 40          FOR F=0 TO 9
 50             G=10*A+E
 60             H=10*B+F
 70             P=G*F
 80             Q=G*B
 90             IF Q<100 THEN 200
100             IF INT(P/10)<>C THEN 200
110             IF Q-10*INT(Q/10)<>D THEN 200
120             PRINT
130             PRINT TAB(6);G
140             PRINT TAB(6);H
150             PRINT TAB(5);"---"
160             PRINT TAB(6);P
170             PRINT TAB(4);Q
180             PRINT TAB(4);"---"
190             PRINT TAB(4);G*H
195             T=T+1
196             GOTO 215
200          NEXT F
210       NEXT E
215    NEXT D
217 NEXT C
219 PRINT T;" IS THE NUMBER OF YEARS."
220 END
```

```
  3 REM   THE  DECADE  OF  THE  1980'S  E2
 10 A=1
 15 B=9
 17 C=9
 20 FOR  D=0  TO  9
 30    FOR  E=0  TO  9
 40      FOR  F=0  TO  9
 50        G=10*A+E
 60        H=10*B+F
 70        P=G*F
 80        Q=G*B
100        IF  INT(P/10)<>C  THEN  200
110        IF  Q-10*INT(Q/10)<>D  THEN  200
112        W=INT(SQR(G*H)+.5)
114        IF  W*W<>G*H  THEN  200
120        PRINT
130        PRINT  TAB(6);G
140        PRINT  TAB(6);H
150        PRINT  TAB(5);"---"
160        PRINT  TAB(6);P
170        PRINT  TAB(4);Q
180        PRINT  TAB(4);"---"
190        PRINT  TAB(4);G*H
195        PRINT  "THE  YEAR  IS  ";A;B;C;D;
    "  WHICH  GIVES  A  FINAL  PRODUCT  OF  ";G*H;
    "  WHICH  IN  TURN  IS  THE  SQUARE  OF  33"
196        GOTO  215
200      NEXT  F
210    NEXT  E
215 NEXT  D
220 END
```

```
  3 REM   THE DECADE OF THE 1980'S E3
  5 T=0
 10 A=1
 15 B=9
 20 FOR C=0 TO 9
 25    FOR D=0 TO 9
 30      FOR E=0 TO 9
 40        FOR F=0 TO 9
 50          G=10*A+E
 60          H=10*B+F
 70          P=G*F
 80          Q=G*B
 88          IF G*H>1000 THEN 200
100          IF INT(P/10)<>C THEN 200
110          IF Q-10*INT(Q/10)<>D THEN 200
120          PRINT
130          PRINT TAB(6);G
140          PRINT TAB(6);H
150          PRINT TAB(5);"---"
160          PRINT TAB(6);P
170          PRINT TAB(4);Q
180          PRINT TAB(4);"---"
190          PRINT TAB(4);G*H
195          T=T+1
200        NEXT F
210      NEXT E
215    NEXT D
217 NEXT C
219 PRINT T;" IS THE NUMBER OF SOLUTIONS."
220 END


  3 REM   SQUARE DIFFERENCES E1
 10 FOR N=1 TO 999
 15    C=0
 20    FOR Y=0 TO N
 30      X=INT(SQR(N+Y*Y)+.5)
 40      IF X*X<>N+Y*Y THEN 60
 55      C=C+1
 60    NEXT Y
 65    IF C=4 THEN 75
 70 NEXT N
 75 PRINT N;" TILES TODAY"
 80 END
```

```
  3 REM   SQUARE DIFFERENCES E2
 10 FOR N=1 TO 99 STEP 2
 15    C=0
 20    FOR Y=0 TO N
 30      X=INT(SQR(N+Y*Y)+.5)
 40      IF X*X<>N+Y*Y THEN 60
 55      C=C+1
 60    NEXT Y
 65    IF C<>1 THEN 70
 67    PRINT N;"      ";
 70 NEXT N
 80 END
```

```
  3 REM   SQUARE DIFFERENCES E3
 10 FOR N=1 TO 999
 15    C=0
 20    FOR Y=0 TO N
 30      X=INT((N+Y*Y*Y)^(1/3)+.5)
 40      IF X*X*X<>N+Y*Y*Y THEN 60
 50      PRINT X;"*";X;"*";X;" - ";Y;"*";Y;"*";Y;" = ";N
 55      C=C+1
 60    NEXT Y
 65    IF C>1 THEN 80
 70 NEXT N
 80 END
```

```
  3 REM    INVERTIBLE NUMBERS E1
  5 C=0
 10 FOR Z=0 TO 999
 15    A$=STR$(Z)
 20    B$=""
 30    L=LEN(A$)
 40    FOR J=L TO 1 STEP -1
 50      D$=MID$(A$,J,1)
 60      IF D$<>"6" AND D$<>"9" THEN 120
 70      IF D$="6" THEN 100
 80      D$="6"
 90      GOTO 130
100      D$="9"
110      GOTO 130
120      IF D$<>"8" AND D$<>"0" THEN 170
130      B$=B$+D$
140    NEXT J
150    IF A$<>B$ THEN 170
155    C=C+1
156    PRINT A$
170 NEXT Z
175 PRINT "THERE ARE ";C;" SELF-INVERTIBLE NUMBERS"
  0 END
```

```
  3 REM   INVERTIBLE NUMBERS E2
  5 C=0
 10 FOR Z=0 TO 9999
 15    A$=STR$(Z)
 20    B$=""
 30    L=LEN(A$)
 40    FOR J=L TO 1 STEP -1
 50       D$=MID$(A$,J,1)
 60       IF D$<>"6" AND D$<>"9" THEN 120
 70       IF D$="6" THEN 100
 80       D$="6"
 90       GOTO 130
100       D$="9"
110       GOTO 130
120       IF D$<>"8" AND D$<>"0" THEN 170
130       B$=B$+D$
140    NEXT J
155    C=C+1
156    IF C=100 THEN 175
170 NEXT Z
175 PRINT "THE ";C;"-TH INVERTIBLE NUMBER IS";A$
180 END


  3 REM   INVERTIBLE NUMBERS E3
  5 C=0
 10 FOR Z=0 TO 999
 15    A$=STR$(Z)
 20    B$=""
 30    L=LEN(A$)
 40    FOR J=L TO 1 STEP -1
 50       D$=MID$(A$,J,1)
 60       IF D$<>"6" AND D$<>"9" THEN 120
 70       IF D$="6" THEN 100
 80       D$="6"
 90       GOTO 130
100       D$="9"
110       GOTO 130
120       IF D$<>"8" AND D$<>"1" AND D$<>"0" THEN 170
130       B$=B$+D$
140    NEXT J
155    C=C+1
156    IF C=100 THEN PRINT "A$=";A$
170 NEXT Z
175 PRINT C;" NUMBERS ARE INVERTIBLE"
180 END
```

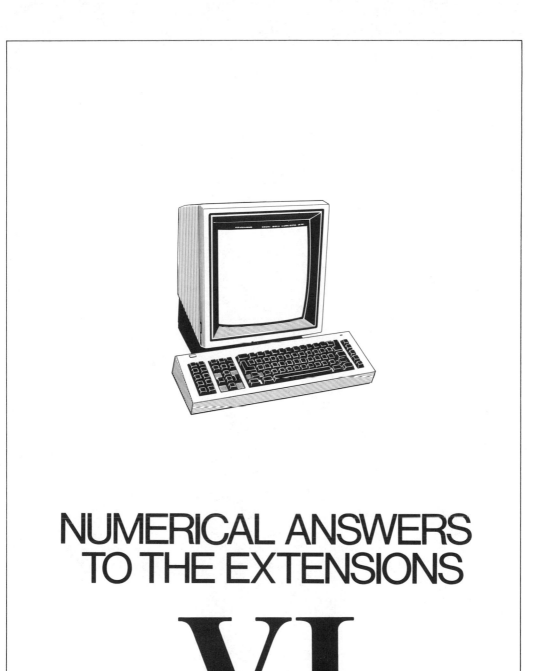

NUMERICAL ANSWERS
TO THE EXTENSIONS

VI

1. WRAPAROUND NUMBERS

1. The first and last years in the twentieth century that are wraparound numbers are 1911 and 1999.
2. There are 193 four-digit wraparound numbers.
3. There are 54 three-digit wraparound numbers.

2. SUMS OF SQUARES

1. 325, 1105.
2. 65.
3. 1729, 1729.

3. DOUBLE DEAL

1. Three times: 5823, 17,469;
   5832, 17,496.
   Four times: 3942, 15,768;
   4392, 17,568;
   5796, 23,184;
   7956, 31,824.
2. 1593, 28,674.
3. 2, 3, 4, 5, 6, 7, 8, 9, 12, 13, 14, 15, 16, 17, 18, 19, 22, 23, 24, 26, 27, 28, 29, 32, 35, 37, 38, 43, 44, 46, 52, 53, 59, 62, 66, 68.

4. RECIPROCAL TRIPLES

1. $1/\sqrt{36} + 1/\sqrt{9} = 1/\sqrt{4}$.
2. $1/2 + 1/2 = 1/1$.
3. $1/6^2 + 1/3^2 + 1/3^2 = 1/2^2$.

5. CHAINS OF CONDENSED NUMBERS

1. 15, 17, 17.
2. These N values end at 1: 10, 13, 19, 23, 28, 31, 32, 44, 49, 68, 70, 79, 82, 86, 91, 94, 97.
3. 44.

6. WHAT'S THE ODOMETER READ?

1. The number on the trip odometer could have been 250, since $250^2 = 62,500$ and $250(2) = 500$, or it could have been 252, since $252^2 = 63,504$ and $252(2) = 504$.

2. The numbers would be

$$128, \text{ since } 128^2 = 16,384 \text{ and } 128(3) = 384$$
$$\text{and } 125, \text{ since } 125^2 = 15,625 \text{ and } 125(5) = 625$$

There are no solutions when the multiple is 4.

3. There are seven solutions, as follows: $100^2 = 10,000$; $250^2 = 62,500$; $376^2 = 141,376$; $500^2 = 250,000$; $600^2 = 360,000$; $625^2 = 390,625$; and $760^2 = 577,600$.

7. ZIP CODES

1. 10,101 is the smallest five-digit palindrome giving a whole number when divided by the sum of its digits, and 94,149 is the largest.

2. The other five are 11,511, 22,122, 44,244, 66,366, and 88,488.

3. 8118 divided by the sum of its digits gives the whole number 451.

8. TEMPERATURE TEASER

1. Dropping the hundreds digit in the Fahrenheit temperatures of 184 and 185 gives Celsius temperatures of 84 and 85, respectively.

2. A Fahrenheit temperature of 82 equals a Celsius temperature of 28. It is the only other two-digit one to give the correct Celsius temperature when its digits are reversed.

3. For a temperature of 125 Fahrenheit, dropping the hundreds digit and reversing the remaining digits gives 52, which is the Celsius equivalent of 125 degrees Fahrenheit.

9. MULTIPLY PERFECT NUMBERS

1. The smallest odd abundant number is 945.

2. These 16 integers are evenly divided by the number of their divisors: 1, 2, 8, 9, 12, 18 , 24, 36, 40, 56, 60, 72, 80, 84, 88, 96.

3. The perfect squares, 1, 4, 9, 16, 25, 36, 49, 64, 81, and 100 have an odd number of divisors.

10. LOCKER NUMBERS

1. There are two sets of possible answers. Bill and Jill's locker numbers could be 220, 2 and 111, 111, respectively, since 220 + 110(2) = 440 and 111 + 110(111) = 12,321. However, because it is not stated that they share a locker, Bill's number is 220 and Jill's is 2.

2. The values of X, Y, and Z are 15, 9, and 3, respectively, since 15 + 10(9) + 100(3) = 405 and 405 − 5 = 400 = 20(20).

3. The values of X, Y, and Z are 10, 11, and 12, respectively, since 10 + 10(11) + 100(12) = 10(11)(12) = 1320.

11. AGE ARRANGEMENTS

1. The ages of the grandchildren are 1, 4, 5, and 8, which form the number 1458.

2. The teenagers' ages are 14 and 19. They form the number 1419.

3. The ages of the cousins are 23, 18, and 4, which form the number 23,184.

12. THE MULTIPLIER EFFECT

1. The five-digit number 21,978 works with the multiplier 4, since 21,978 × 4 = 87,912.

2. The other is 23,958 with the multiplier 7, since 12,903 × 7 = 90,321.

3. There are none.

13. REVERSE AND ADD

1. The process does produce palindromes for all two-digit numbers. However, the numbers 89 and 98 produce the 13-digit palindrome 8,813,200,023,188, which is too large to fit in a single memory location on your computer.

2. The number 19 is the smallest to require two additions to produce a palindrome. The smallest requiring three and four additions are 59 and 69, respectively.

3. No. Single-digit numbers and many three-digit numbers lead to palindromes that are not multiples of 11. (It is true, however, that each two-digit number leads to a palindrome that is a multiple of 11.)

14. DIFFERENT DIGITS

1. The five three-digit numbers with repeated digits are 100, 112, 200, 400, and 500.
2. In total, there are 4536 four-digit numbers with no repeated digits.
3. There are 29 four-digit numbers with no repeated digits, with the needed property. The smallest is 1053; the largest, 9720.

15. POSITIVE DIFFERENCES

1. There are 16 sets that require eight repetitions before reaching 0, 0, 0, 0. They are: 0149, 0589, 0941, 0985, 1094, 1490, 4109, 4901, 5098, 5890, 8509, 8905, 9014, 9058, 9410, 9850.
2. Five repetitions are needed, regardless of the size of the first number.
3. Five repetitions are needed, regardless of the size of the first number.

16. HOW MANY JELLY BEANS?

1. The maximum number is 9924 beans.
2. Maxwell was born in 1918. His grandson was born in 1978.
3. No numbers of less than 10,000 are satisfied by the conditions in set c.

17. ARRANGING SOLDIERS IN SQUARES

1. The value $N = 29$ gives 96,059,600 soldiers.
2. When $N = 3, 8, 15, 24, 35, \ldots$, the number of soldiers equals N. In general, whenever N is one less than a square, the number of soldiers equals N.
3. For $Y = 2$, the first five values of N are 2, 6, 12, 20, and 30. In general, the ith value of N is $i(i + 1)$.

18. THE DECADE OF THE 1980s

1. There are 57 years in the twentieth century which give solutions. Note that the number of years that give solutions will not be the same as the number of solutions if some year(s) have more than one solution. For example, explore the nineteenth century.

2. The year 1999 gives a perfect square $1089 = 33^2$. No year gives a product that is a perfect cube. The years 1939 and 1976 give products of 1023 and 1330, respectively, which are one less than the perfect square $1024 = 32^2$ and the perfect cube $1331 = 11^3$.

3. There are 11 years for which a solution exists. They are 1900, 1909, 1910, 1920, 1930, 1940, 1950, 1960, 1970, 1980, and 1990.

19. SQUARE DIFFERENCES

1. The smallest number that is the difference of two squares in four ways is 96.

2. There are 25 odd numbers of less than 100 that can be written as the difference of two squares in only one way. They include all the primes between 1 and 100: 1, 3, 5, 7, 11, 13, 17, 19, 23, 29, 31, 37, 41, 43, 47, 53, 59, 61, 67, 71, 73, 79, 83, 89, and 97.

3. The numbers of less than 100 that can be written as the difference of two cubes are 1, 7, 8, 19, 26, 27, 37, 56, 61, 63, 64, 91, and 98.

20. INVERTIBLE NUMBERS

1. There are six self-invertible numbers between 100 and 999. They are: 609, 689, 808, 888, 906, and 986.

2. The 100th invertible number is 6809.

3. When 1 is included as an invertible digit, the 100th invertible number is 899.

INDEX
OF COMPUTER PROBLEM-SOLVING TECHNIQUES

*Problem 0 is Mad Mary's Problem, in Part I, "How to Use This Book."

Technique	*Problems*
Testing for equality	0*, 1, 3, 6, 7, 8, 11, 12, 13, 15, 16, 17, 18, 20
Testing for integers	4, 14, 15, 20
Testing for squares	4, 10, 16, 17
Testing whether a counter equals a specific number	2, 15, 19
Testing whether a counter has exceeded a specific number	5, 13